"I am very impressed with _____ E books as a rule, but I foun_____ ve of inspiring information ab___ ___ ___story, complexity, life changing effects and long term research concerning the NDE. I believe that this book will lead many non-believers in the NDE to take another look at this world-wide phenomenon and also help many NDE'ers to assimilate their own experience in a deeper way."

—Mellen-Thomas Benedict, Researcher/Inventor in the field of Biophotonics/Cellular Communication, Near-Death Experiencer

"PMH Atwater, a leading NDE researcher and experiencer, sums up all she has learned about NDEs, life, death—and God—in this stunning and revelatory book of wisdom teachings stemming from her many years of work in the field. Even people generally familiar with NDEs will find much to treasure in this illuminating book written in PMH's inimitable warm and winning style."

—Kenneth Ring, Ph.D., author with Sharon Cooper of *Mindsight: Near-Death and Out-Of-Body Experiences in the Blind*, and with Evelyn Elsaesser-Valarino of *Lessons From the Light: What We Can Learn from the Near-Death Experience*

"Atwater makes a compelling case for the existence of God, going where few researchers have gone before: meeting God while in the midst of a near-death experience. Her many insights into the realm beyond, and those of others whom she has interviewed, provide what may well be a picture window into a soul's journey back to its maker. Her writing is clear, her reporting thorough, her arguments crisp, her message compelling. Life has value, life has reason, life has meaning."

—Sidney Kirkpatrick, award-winning documentary filmmaker and best-selling author

"A tireless researcher and a prolific writer, PMH Atwater has in many books and numerous lectures shared glimpses of the ineffable which she has gleaned from her own near-death experiences and from the hundreds of experiencers of all ages whom she has interviewed during decades of research. In this new work, her own deep passion and personal mission blend seamlessly with the findings of other experts in the field to make for an extremely powerful read and a testimony that God is truly at the center of all near-death experiences."

—Sherry Steiger and Brad Steiger , authors of *Real Miracles, Divine Intervention,* and *Feats of Incredible Survival*

"PMH Atwater is masterful in her new book, *The Experience of God*, as she interlocks the science of near-death experience and the undeniable fact of eternal soul consciousness. Readers will find a remarkable plethora of validation that we are divine in body and spirit at all times, with purpose."

—Dr. Linda Backman, author of *Bringing Your Soul to Light: Healing through Past Lives and the Time Between* and *The Evolving Soul: Spiritual Healing through Past Life Exploration*

"In reading P.M.H. Atwater's latest book, *Dying to Know You*, I found myself being led on an amazing journey detailing what many experience in what is the most profound mystery of life . . . what lies beyond death. Written in a delightful style that keeps the pages turning, Atwater shares from her extensive research remarkable case studies of those who have crossed over and returned to share their visions and experiences. The overwhelming evidence is sure to invite skeptics to question their conclusions on the subject. The wisdom, clarity, and insight interspersed throughout the book are profound and when I finished, I was left wanting more. From her own

NDE she quotes, "Always there is life. We cannot escape ourselves or what we have built ourselves to be, as death ends
nothing but the physical body we wear. The soul, who we are,
continues." A powerful message of hope and clarity, Atwater's
book is a must read that can assist many to see their lives and
the lives of others in a totally new way, a gift so needed at this
time in history. Thank you, PMH."

— Margaretta Mcilvaine is the founder of Bridge Between The
Worlds Retreat Center in Keswick , Virginia, where she hosts and
conducts numerous workshops on healing and spirituality. For
more information: *www.bridgebetweentheworlds.org*

"Since Raymond Moody's book came out in the '70s I have
been reading—absorbing in my heart—all the book I could
about NDEs. However, it was not until I discovered one
Atwater's books that I realized that when I nearly died as a
child, that was exactly what happened to me. I was profoundly
affected by it! I contacted Atwater around the year 2000, and
she gave me an in-depth understanding of some very disturbing and shameful 'hauntings' that had bothered me.

This book is a power-house. The power from her own
NDEs shines through her very words giving us a summary of
35 years of NDE research. She manages at the same time to
give me as a reader a mirror to understand my own very personal experiences."

—Aud Marit Viken Esbensen, MBA, Oslo, Norway, Family Con-
stellation Teach and Guide, Economist Researcher

"I'm stunned! I can only digest a little bit at a time. You have
put into words the impossible. Everything I 'know' in the
deepest sense of my heart, that I cannot adequately describe,

you've written as if it's ethereal and words don't translate. You've done a great, wonderful job!"

—Greg Smith, originator of Hollywood Grave Line Tours, Proof Reader, Waiter, Near-Death Experiencer

"*Dying to Know You* is a magnificent gift—the distillation, the essence, the perfume of a life fully lived and examined—but not just a life, but three near-dyings as well. Journeying through life into death without the wisdom and experience of a guide such as P.M.H. Atwater is as unwise as an expedition without a compass.

This book is a treasure. It ranks among the loftiest expressions in modern survival literature. It expresses succinctly a spirituality anchored in personal experience and empiricism. It restores meaning and hope in a world in which they are in short supply. It is rare that such a huge cache of wisdom is packed in so few pages. And I almost forgot to mention: this book is a reader's delight."

—Larry Dossey , MD, author of *One Mind: How Our Individual Mind Is Part of a Greater Consciousness and Why It Matters*

DYING
TO KNOW YOU

Also by P.M.H. Atwater

*Children of the Fifth World: A Guide to the
Coming Changes in Human Consciousness* (2012)

*Near-Death Experiences, The Rest of the Story: What They Teach Us
about Living and Dying and Our True Purpose* (2011)

I Died Three Times in 1977—The Complete Story (2010)

*The Big Book of Near Death Experiences:
The Ultimate Guide to What Happens When We Die* (2007)

Beyond the Indigo Children (2005)

We Live Forever (2004)

The New Children and Near-Death Experiences (2003)

Coming Back to Life (2001)

The Complete Idiot's Guide to Near-Death Experiences (1999)

Children of the New Millennium (1999)

Future Memory (1999)

Goddess Runes (1996)

Beyond the Light (1994)

DYING
TO KNOW YOU

Proof of God

in the

Near-Death Experience

P. M. H. ATWATER, L.H.D.

RAINBOW RIDGE
BOOKS

Cover and interior design by Frame25 Productions
Cover photograph © djgis c/o Shutterstock.com

Published by:
Rainbow Ridge Books, LLC
140 Rainbow Ridge Road
Faber. Virginia 22938
434-361-1723

If you are unable to order this book from your local
bookseller, you may order directly from the distributor.

Square One Publishers, Inc.
115 Herricks Road
Garden City Park, NY 11040
Phone: (516) 535-2010
Fax: (516) 535-2014
Toll-free: 877-900-BOOK

Visit the author at:
www.pmhatwater.com

Library of Congress Cataloging-in-Publication Data applied for.

ISBN 978-1-937907-28-0

10 9 8 7 6 5 4 3 2 1

Printed on acid-free paper in Canada

CONTENTS

*The world is full of people who
have never, since childhood,
met an open doorway
with an open mind.*
—E. B. White

Dedicated to the thousands of people
who have shared their heart and soul
with me; and to the man who gives
love's blessings with each touch . . .
my husband Terry.

Special thanks to Mellen-Thomas
Benedict who witnessed my search for
guidance in writing this book; and to
Father Thaddaeus Hardenbrook of the
Greek Orthodox Church, Felton,
California, who opened the door to
the miracles inside my prayer.

FOREWORD

On a flight to San Francisco, April 19, 2013, the unexpected happened. What I mean by that is, an energy in front of my face began writing a book. First came the title page, then the table of contents, front quotes, outline for eleven chapters, and backmatter. This was energy—just air that seemed possessed of its own consciousness. No exotic or spooky being, no voices, no channeling, no vision. Just energy, in front of my face, writing a book. Very strange.

After a while I took pen to paper and wrote the thing down. This was uncomfortable because it made no sense. I refused to accept the manner of this intrusion; still, the energy keep writing. Words and ideas kept pouring forth. There seemed to be no way to stop what was happening. Days became weeks in a non-stop circuit of talks, workshops, and travels I was committed to do. One such foray took me through Felton, California. Funky town. Almost hidden next to the large Antique Barn was a Greek Orthodox Church. I made a bee-line for it and the solace of prayer. I needed guidance. Kneeling, with my forehead to the floor, I heard a soft grandfatherly voice say: "Hush child, hush child. Now, do your work." The message spoke to my soul. I could now trust what was happening. This book is a tickler, not heavy on research as most of my others, not anything I would ever write by choice or design. Nope. Its purpose is simply to allow the heart inside near-death experiences to speak. That heart, our heart of hearts, needs to be heard.

The market is crowded today with gripping tomes about near-death experiences. Cases of verifiable details and corroboration not only from loved ones, but from the medical establishment itself. A number of them are now bestsellers. People seem unable to hear enough, read enough, learn enough . . . from those who have passed through death's doorway and returned.

I've been on the cutting edge of this phenomenon since 1978, one of the pioneers to emerge in this new field of study. My research base numbers nearly 4,000 adults and children. Ten books contain my findings, some of which have since been clinically verified, including in the Dutch study published in *Lancet Medical Journal*, 12-15-01. My *The Big Book of Near-Death Experiences* is considered the encyclopedia of the phenomenon worldwide; *Near-Death Experiences: The Rest of The Story* sums up over 33 years of questioning and probing, checking, and rechecking, along with a decade I spent before I died investigating the mystical path. What I have rarely mentioned is that when I began my research of near-death, I had never heard of Raymond Moody or his book, *Life After Life*. Elisabeth Kübler Ross, whom I met at O'Hare Airport outside of Chicago, told me about such episodes as she validated the three near-death experiences I had had within three months time in 1977. She called me a near-death survivor, but never said a word about Raymond or his book. Hardly returned from dying myself, I began my work, a research project I was told to do by a voice of other-worldly power that spoke to me during my third episode. "Test Revelation," it said. "You are to do the research. One book for each death." Books two and three were named, not book one. I was shown what was to be in each book but not how to do the job or how long it would take me. Meeting Elisabeth at O'Hare gave me the strength and the determination to begin. That soft grandfatherly voice at the Greek Orthodox Church gave me the courage to go back and finish the job—of letting the heart's truth ring out through jumbles of individual narratives and research findings.

What has been missing from my work, from everyone else's work, from personal stories, from those who interpret personal stories, from experts in religion and spirituality, from the news media, the scientists, the grief-stricken, and the born again . . . is the voice of the collective . . . *inside* what we all seek to describe. That voice, the sum of the many, speaks like a thunderclap.

What lies at the heart of near-death experiences? A God that in ways beyond description, smiles at you. Not the God of holy writ, but a Sourceplace—an all-encompassing Oneness, Allness, that, as It breathes, moves skin and bark and wings and stars and babes and rivers and comets and dreams and faces . . . as well as the mustard on your hotdog. The book you have before you releases that collective voice, the sum of millions of people—worldwide—who speak as one.

To make certain this is so, the "air-that-is-conscious" returned ten months later, just before publication, to rearrange a few things and add two more chapters. This surprised me. Perhaps that added material will surprise you, too.

1

MISSION

God is.

Death isn't.

The typical near-death experiencer wants to shout words like this to a deluded humanity, to stand on a rooftop and scream them until the sound of their passion fades into the cacophony of cars and people busy chasing the louder voices of need, hunger, and desire. Who notices some crazy fool spouting off messages about a supreme being and an ecstasy to be found beyond the finality of death? Who'd believe such nonsense?

You can't stop them, though. By the thousands they come, in growing numbers they come—now numbering in the tens of millions—spreading across continents and oceans. People in ways unique to each are discovering worlds beyond death . . . beyond the grind of metal cracking bone, shots ringing in ears, the pounding pain of a heart in crisis, screams of a mother dying as her baby breathes new air . . . through the juggernaut of fear and panic experiencers of the near-death phenomenon are flung "elsewhere."

As life ends, life shifts.

"Elsewhere" becomes a destination.

Whether a brief trip out of the body experienced by an earthquake victim in China, or a gathering of angels surrounding a Montana bull rider with a snapped neck, or a bag-boy crushed between two cars at a grocery store in Georgia shown all of history from beginning to end as he fought for each breath, or with a child bitten by an asp in northern France miraculously healed by a Lady in White . . . makes no difference who or what or when or how . . . without warning, suddenly, experiencers see beyond eyes, hear beyond ears, smell beyond odor, feel beyond touch, know things beyond the grasp of brain or memory—theirs or anyone else's. Not everyone who breaches the borderlands of death has a near-death experience. But for those who do, a sense of mission intrudes upon all else.

The majority of near-death experiencers return with a single, overriding sense of mission: *share your story*. Tell others, as many as you can for as long as you can. And, they are infused with this truth: death does not end life. A body is something we wear. They come back convinced you, me, all of us, are not our body. We are not our name, social security number, or the face we see in the mirror. Neither are we defined by our family, our religion, our job, our station in life, our money or lack of it. We are more than that. The body that appears to be us is a loaner. We have it for as long as needed, then it sloughs away.

The realization is: it's no accident we died and are back again. On some level, somehow, what happened was needed—as if "a wakeup call." How do you share this? What will people think when you tell them? Will they believe you? The fear of rejection silences most. Who among us can go through life being labeled a nut, having people poke fun, or fending off accusations of possible drug use or imagination gone wild?

The puzzle of mission is two-fold: most of us were sent back and told we had a mission to perform or a job yet to do—it wasn't our time. Others popped back into their bodies, sans choice. Seldom is anyone actually told the specifics of what their job is. We learn that life is purposeful and that we must finish what we came for, the path set in motion with our birth. But that's about it.

Mission: tell your story, do your job (even if you don't know what that job is).

The majority long to return to this elsewhere place. Life is better there. Colors are brighter. Sounds are clearer. You move with thought and with a sense of "feel." It's a spiritual place because of the love that infuses every inch of it and the wide-open acceptance that greets you. You recognize the place. No matter who you are or where you've been or what you've done with your life, when you die, you're home again. That sense of familiarity grabs you and won't let go.

The longing to return runs head-on into the reality of mission. You want to go back but you can't. Even the lure of suicide seldom tempts. The grief of not knowing or forgetting what your mission is motivates you to keep trying. Somehow you will be led to your job. You know you will. Your mission awaits.

I was one of the lucky ones; my mission spelled out for me during my third episode by what I came to call "The Voice Like None Other." Swinging into action after I revived didn't happen, though. What folks forget is that the majority of near-death experiences emerge from violence or trauma. You have a body to rebuild afterward and questions to answer. What just happened? What does it mean?

Plus every kind of why you can think of.

In my case I had to relearn how to stand, crawl, walk, climb stairs, run, tell the difference between left and right, see properly, hear properly, and rebuild all my belief systems. Exercises and classes were daily fare, sometimes hourly, for a year and a half. Heaven for me then was that sun-shiny day in downtown Boise, Idaho, when I could run an entire city block and there was no pain and I didn't fall down.

A house I had owned barely six months sold in a cash-out. My youngest went to live with her father. The other two were grown and gone. I stuffed into my Ford Pinto bathroom, kitchen, and bed supplies, a ladder, vacuum cleaner, files, canned goods, some clothes, and family photos. After saying goodbye to my parents, I left Idaho, driving first to the coast-line of southern California to watch the sun set silver over the Pacific, then zigzagging cross country to fulfill childhood dreams of places I had always wished to see, arriving at last at the Chesapeake's mouth where I gazed enraptured as the sun rose golden over the Atlantic.

Here I began . . . giving talks, knocking on doors, finding experiencers wherever I went. They seemed to be waiting for someone like me, someone who would listen without judgment.

The classical model of the near-death experience never informed my work, nor have I been constrained by so-called "scientific protocols." I am simply a cop's kid who spent a lot of time in a police station and learned all I could about the investigative process. Since over 70 percent of the medical techniques used today are based on the type of observation and analysis I conducted, I have always felt my research was just as good as anyone else's.

I quickly learned during my labors that no single account, no matter how amazing or awesome or unbelievable, speaks with the power of the many. It is that collective voice, theirs, mine, that is woven into the pages that follow . . . *a collective voice that opens wide the heart inside such experiences . . . to reveal a God beyond imagining.*

The idea we have of God or Allah or Deity *isn't big enough.* We've fashioned our idea of Creator in our own image, instead of realizing that we, the created, are bigger, too.

2

GOD

Face it: easily 90 to 95 percent of near-death experiencers, not just in my study, return absolutely convinced that God exists. Whether atheist, agnostic, purveyor of fairy tales, or avid worshipper, watch the experiencer's face change when someone mentions God . . . a special calmness spreads, a kind of "glow," as if to affirm *all is well*. The rest return unsure that anything like the God "good books" deem holy ever could have existed, that "something else" must be true, perhaps another reality-factor altogether. But get this—atheists who come back still atheists are happier and healthier than before as if suddenly possessed of a "new gospel," that of forgiveness and compassion. They claim no god, yet act as if touched by something surreal.

Name? So, what do we call the God of those who survive death or nearly die and return with narratives that challenge age-old beliefs?

Is it true that Christian near-death experiencers describe the God they saw or sensed on the other side of death's curtain as the one found in the Bible? With Muslims, is the Allah they find the same as the one who brought forth the Qur'an? Do Jews greet the Elohim of the Torah? Native Americans, the Creator God of their nation's history? Do Buddhists discover a Greater Force of Energy that stretches even their traditions?

Yes and no.

There is no question that experiencers describe what they saw during their episode in the language style they are the most familiar with. Some even go out of their way to find words that "fit" what is more acceptable in their culture. Be realistic here . . . what other words could they use? Listen carefully for fumbles, though. What they don't say reveals more than what they do. That's because near-death experiences are ineffable. Words just don't cut it. How does anyone describe the indescribable?

And then there's that question of gender.

Adult experiencers hardly ever describe God as a man. Some do speak of a father-figure and use the pronoun "he." Yet any sense of maleness comes across more as a "habit-phrase." What I mean by that is throughout the world's various cultures and religions, power/strength/enormity-of-being has been and still is associated with maleness, whether historically accurate or not. Adult experiencers juggle this. Although they may still use words familiar to them, there's no real indicator that they continue to believe what they once did. Certainly some do, claiming their experience proves their holy book right and all other teachings false. The rest, the majority, show signs of expanded viewpoints, enhanced intelligence, deeper levels of understanding.

Kids are different. To a child experiencer, God is "father" or "grandfather" or "lord." As a father-figure, God is all love, all blessing, all kindness. Seldom does a child question God, but occasionally one will. And they'll wrap that question into a "kinda" test: "Is that what you really look like?" Answers are amazingly consistent worldwide: father-figure God instantly bursts into a huge, bright ball of All-Encompassing Light (same thing happens should the questioner be an adult). Children often test angels with the same question, and get the same result . . . with a twist . . . an angel's light is not as powerful or as big or as bright as God's.

I have yet to find either adult or child who experienced God as female or as a mother-figure . . . except through the presence of a special dark or black light. This surprising truism is but one of many . . . that connects the subject of God with the subject of light. You can't talk about one without the other, because the real subject is power, a power beyond reckoning.

Now that we've admitted this, the "lid's" off the subject.

Fact: the vast majority of adults in any country see God/Allah/Deity as a formless, shapeless brilliance so powerful and so strong and so magnificent that Its Beingness is felt as if a power voltage equivalent to 10,000 suns. You're instantly "fried," yet there is no pain, nothing negative or hurtful. The presence of this Light is associated with Deity. And this Light knows your name, knows all about you, can converse with you, answer questions, and give guidance. There's nothing this Light doesn't know, especially the things you don't. And this Light loves you and forgives you, but can be cryptic in the giving of mission and what next needs to be done to heal, help, and uplift self and others. You cannot fool this Light, nor can you hide or pretend in Its Presence. Other-worldly guides and guardians, angels and greeters of every stripe, can appear, too, and "fill in the blanks" for you if you missed anything.

They can contribute additional advice and wisdom, but that Central Light most assuredly takes Center Stage. No "messing around." What needs to be said, is.

Besides hues and shades of color that can appear and disappear, the Light of God/Allah/Deity is dominant and seems triune in nature. Children are usually specific about this. Their descriptions combined with that of adults go like this:

- *Primary Light* (luminous) is seen as a raw radiance, a piercing power so awesome in its strength that prolonged contact makes experiencers feel as if they are about to explode.

- *Dark or Black Light* (can have purple tinges) is felt to be velvety and warm, a safe haven most often associated with miraculous healings and unexplainable genius (seldom ever associated with evil, although some can perceive it that way).

- *Bright or White Light* (can have silver or yellow/gold tinges) an almost blinding brilliance that emanates unconditional love and knowingness and peace.

Child experiencers sometimes refer to the bright light as "Father Light," the dark or black light as "Mother Light," and the primary, luminous light as "God's Light." They are quite adamant that Father Light and Mother Light come from God's Light. Throughout the many decades of my work, I have noticed that the biggest jumps in intelligence afterward and the most remarkable healings that occurred could usually be traced to either being in that dark or black light or having that type of light come to you as if in the personage of an angel of mercy or a cloud-like ball. Yes, there are narratives from experiencers who found themselves in a hellish or frightening environment that was filled with darkness. Never once were these exceptions associated with anything warm, velvety, or compassionate, or as a type of safe haven where healing occurs.

I suspect there may be degrees of voltage with these lights, how strong or weak they are, how are they felt, what comes from being bathed in each. And I do mean voltage, as there is an undeniable electrical component to near-death experiences and the aftereffects which spring from them. Here's a "for instance": the electromagnetic field in and around experiencers alters afterward, with displays of electrical sensitivity becoming commonplace.

Pardon me, but isn't that what near-death, mystical, spiritual, and religious experiencers have claimed for centuries? That the Light of Enlightenment is actually that, literally a waking up to Light, an illumination of Light, a reunification with The One True Light. And there are groups, isms and schisms, that decree how people can reach such a state of enlightened knowingness. The rules are many, the pathways numerous, still, the goal is always the same . . . union with the source of your being . . . God!

Is that what a near-death experience is? Is it another way among many to discover the spiritual and connect or reconnect with the numinous?

As a researcher, I can assure you that any type of near-death experience can be life changing. But as an experiencer, I can positively affirm that being bathed in Light on the other side of death *is more than life changing.*

That Light is the very essence, the heart and soul, the all-consuming consummation of ecstatic ecstasy. It is indeed a million suns of compressed love dissolving everything unto Itself, annihilating thought and cell, vaporizing humanness and history, into the one great brilliance of all that is and all that ever was and all that ever will be.

You know the Light is God.

No one has to tell you.

You know.

You can no longer believe in God afterward, for belief implies doubt. There is no more doubt. None. You now *know* God. And you know that you know. And you're never the same again.

And you know who you are . . . a child of God, a cell in The Greater Body, an extension of The One Force, an expression from The One Mind. No more can you forget your identity, or deny or ignore or pretend it away.

There is One, and you are of The One.

One.

The Light does this to you. It cradles your soul in the heart of its pulse-beat and fills you with love shine. And you melt away as the "you" you think you are, reforming as the "YOU" you really are, and you are reborn because at last you remember.

Although not everyone speaks of God when they return from death's door as I have here, the majority do. And almost to a person they begin to make references to oneness, allness, isness as the directive presence behind and within and beyond all things.

I've noticed that although God never changes, God is forever changing. As our perceptions alter, as personal experience trumps what we thought we knew, the name of God can and often does undergo a "make-over."

The most commonly used names for God after such an intensely-felt experience of other-worldly light, whether during a near-death experience or from some other, similar type of transformation, are: Mother-Father-God (in an attempt to overcome gender issues); Core, Source, Light, Presence (as a way to emphasize the truth of God's existence); The All, One, The Force, Universal Essence, The Greater Good, Supreme Being, That Which Knows Itself, Divine Principle (an enlargement of viewpoint).

Personally, I still use the title "God" because I am comfortable doing so, but I no longer have any sense of he, him, father, mother, god, or goddess. God to me is genderless. Overtime, those who experienced death or nearly died come to regard "God" as nameless "Presence"—existent beyond what words can tell, a conscious intelligence and creative principle so great that It envelops and permeates all levels, all things, all possibilities, all potential, all aspects of creation, all belief systems.

3

SOUL

Yes, we have one . . . a soul . . . the real us, who we really are. Call it Higher Self or Greater Self, our soul is finer and lighter of substance than our physical body. It permeates the physical while being ever "plugged in" or connected to God Presence. Bodies are visible, souls are not—at least not to those with regular vision. After you die and come back, your vision tends to expand and accelerate, along with that of your other faculties.

Soul and body are distinctly different with unique roles to play. The personality we develop while in human form enables us to "learn and grow" from each success or failure; while the soul we are carries within it the original "blueprint" of our true identity. We don't get "lost" during the living of life unless we ignore our soul's promptings.

Once we recognize this, it is hugely important that we remember.

Although the curriculum of life is "writ over there," carrying out that curriculum and developing the "muscles" we need to fulfill it, is accomplished "here" —in a body on planet earth. It's like, how can we possibly inherit "the kingdom of God" (as promised in most Holy Books, mystical and spiritual writings), if we don't first understand the responsibilities and duties of "stewardship?" We need to be fully here, in order to stay over "there" once we arrive.

Our soul is what keeps us on track.

And the quickest way to access our soul is through prayer and meditation.

Think *spiritual.*

Vast numbers of experiencers consider near-death states to be *spiritual experiences.* They refer to them that way because of what happened and because of how that gave them more of a personal connection to God, to the divinity within them— as them. The difference between us as an embodied personality and us as a soul "hanging out in a body" eventually fades. Yet the desire to "keep in touch" continues. Our many parts and possibilities merge into one once we relax into a regimen of prayer and meditation, or something similar.

Oh, by the way, we are larger outside the body than inside. Our energy as a mass enlarges and becomes stronger when unrestrained by the confines of our physical body. Souls seem to possess immense voltage strength and a certain "feel" to the potential they have. Yet by standards of physical size, souls appear as nothing more than teeny tiny sparks.

I hear this again and again from experiencers, how big their size becomes once freed of physical form, an enlargement of size that can be physically felt as it occurs. You're still you but suddenly you are more than before, and freed to move around without hindrance—should a wall be in the way. The freedom of not having a heavy body to lug around is nothing short of remarkable. Going back inside that body means a tight squeeze. You have to shrink to fit and that can take some doing, as well as readjusting to weight.

Questions of soul size, how big we are as a soul, bring to mind a study that was done in the early 1900s by Dr. Duncan MacDougall. With patients' permission, he positioned those who were about to die on a large scale. Each time one expired, there was a measurable loss of between one half and three quarters of an ounce of body mass. Later, a team of five physicians at a Massachusetts hospital replicated Dr. MacDougall's work. Over a span of six years, their tests showed an average loss of about one ounce at the moment of death, no matter the individual. Why so small? Well, if you consider how much information an average microchip can carry, a whole ounce could indeed be the carrier of seemingly limitless material. Look again at the tests, though, and ask yourself: Why was anything lost at all? Each time? Consistently? As if around an ounce was the actual weight of the soul?

Thomas Edison believed in life after death. He was convinced that the soul was made of "life units"—indestructible, microscopic particles that could rearrange into any form while retaining full memory and personality. He died before he could finish building the machine that he was convinced could detect them.

Compare these experiments to the present. Self-declared ghost hunters are using electromagnetic field (EMF) detectors to find certain electrical elements at sites of active hauntings. They claim that when ghosts are present EMF readings are higher than what the device can produce by itself.

Life units? Electrical interference patterns? Voltage meters? Are ghosts lost or wayward souls or remnants of souls or leftover tracings of what once was a soul?

Near-death research cannot answer these questions, but it does address puzzles of "appearance."

Hardly ever do experiencers look back to see how they appeared once freed of physical form. Their primary concerns are "what happened" and "where am I." Sometimes, though, either right away or later into their episode, a few do take a peek at their own form . . . maybe by raising an arm or sticking out a leg.

And a few actually see themselves—size, shape, coloration, density—everything as before. No change. Still, there are those who have quite another type of "showing." They appeared filmy and vaporous rather than human-like, similar to a fog, or consistent with plasma having density akin to that of smoke. Descriptive words like ethereal or brilliant are frequently used, or seeing one's self as a spark of holy fire. Narratives like these suggest that Dr. MacDougall and Thomas Edison may have been on the right track. Combine this with stories of those who visit India and report that for a distance from funeral pyres, patches of a filmy substance lie about as if discarded. Locals say the discards are what is left after a soul is released from its dying body. ("Ectoplasma" is the name for this substance; term also used to describe what psychic mediums produce while in trance states.)

When queried about what other people looked like who populated their near-death episode, almost to a person experiencers agreed: like they always did, only somewhat brighter, younger, healthier, and healed of any deformity.

Refer to "Hotshots from Hell," found in *The Big Book of Near-Death Experiences*. In a nutshell, the story goes like this. A group of firefighters were trapped by a quick change in wind direction. Oxygen evaporated. The "hotshots" collapsed. As he fell, Jake thought, "This is it. I am going to die." And with that thought, he found himself in the air looking down on his body lying in a trench. He looked around and saw the other firefighters also standing above their bodies in the air. One of Jake's crew members had been born with a defective foot. As he came out of his body, Jake looked at him and said, "Look, Jose, your foot is straight."

None of the crew was able to say anything or talk with one another until after fire investigators interviewed them. Each told the same story—of seeing the others rise from their bodies and hover mid-air before they continued on with a scenario similar in kind to the universal pattern of near-death states. This group saw each other plainly and fully. And each confirmed . . . the deformed man was seen as healed once he left his body.

Dramatic? Yes. Yet this case is typical in how people see themselves and others once "out and over." Descriptions given depict younger, healthier, happier versions of those they see. None of this, though, matches or explains what you hear when experiencers talk about "self." Other people are easily recognized once you've left the confines of your physical body. But, you?

Some say yes, you look the same, or maybe just a little better. Others, a whole lot of others, tell a very different story.

Even though experiencers readily identify themselves as a soul, there is an awareness, something akin to an understanding, that the soul, their soul, everyone's soul, has a will of its own—an agenda apart from personality. It's like we move from "the little" to "the larger" once we cross over.

This understanding is not necessarily automatic. What we went through in our lives, what we believed, our passions, joys, and grief, take time to reassess. Emotions can overwhelm at first. We awaken in stages to the degree that we can handle. The discovery that we are more than we think we are is like a giant whoosh of fresh air. Ah-h-h-h-h.

As this truth unfolds, deep calls to deep. Puny notions of humanhood and everything that we once thought really mattered dissolve into waves of longing as thought and memory reposition themselves to capture even glimpses of greater how's and why's. The soul knows. As a soul, we know. Near-death experiences and other transformational states like them help us to remember, to get back in touch with what we forgot.

That sweep of discovery, undulating as if wave-like, sometimes flashing or sparkling as if a power grid or circuit board of energetic light particles, is the spirit of us . . . the breath of us.

Many adult experiencers claimed that during their episode it seemed as though the whole universe and all of creation were breathing. To them, this breath came to represent the stirring of God's Thought, as it reverberated throughout an ever-expanding field of conscious awareness, what we think of as creation. Child experiencers were more plain spoken: "Spirit is everywhere, like air, and it breathes, but not like our nose does. That means everything breathes. I do. You do. So does God. God's Breath is what keeps the universe alive."

If you go back in history, "spirit" originally meant "essence" or "breath." You can make word-plays out of this. As examples, when we say we're being spiritual, the inference is that we have chosen to live in "the fullness of breath's essence." When we speak of spirituality, we are actually describing "the source from whence the pureness of breath comes." Spirit realms are "source places of pure essence." Spirit beings are "visitors or emissaries from source places of pure essence." The stunning surprise for me came when "Holy Spirit" was re-examined in this manner. Some biblical scholars have done this. The translation? "The Breath of God Breathing."

The sensation that the universe and everything in it is alive and breathing underscores the testimony of almost every experiencer of intensely-felt, transformative states of consciousness, no matter how caused. Experiencers come to realize that spirit and breath and essence weave together into a single fabric, a tapestry we call "existence," a tapestry we can appreciate if we reduce its scope to the basic function of breathing in and breathing out.

Take a deep breath.

That deep breath calms your nerves and perks up your brain. It's not just the added oxygen we take into our lungs that does that, but the circulation of that oxygen. Breath movement is the most common way we have for determining aliveness. Experiencers say: *it's the same thing on the other side of death's curtain.*

The universe is alive and it breathes. Spirit is that breath. The Breath of God Breathing is the holy fire that enlivens and energizes the soul and all created things.

4

LIFE AND DEATH

The wonder of being alive shines with a light all its own, reminding us that plain, ordinary life, is our baseline, our "scoreboard" of gains and losses, what we do with the life we have.

Near-death experiences return us to that baseline: breath, movement, sight, sound, spoken word or passing thought, decisions, vows, relationships, promises, touch, tears, emotions, dreams.

Life has value. Life has reason. Life has purpose.

Just entering the womb, hearing and feeling the reality of "mother," birthing into an air world that enables us to learn and in the process of that learning grow muscles, the kind of muscles that prove there is a curriculum at hand—a curriculum that is somehow "chosen"—is more important than any of us think. Where we go in life depends on what turn we take or is taken for us, our choices or lack of them. Strangely, *the how of living* is what enhances or diminishes that curriculum. Always the curriculum. Known or unknown, our job, our mission, the reason for our birth, is part of an infinitely large field of potential, a shimmering consciousness that both includes and transcends us. It's why we're here . . . earth . . . the "school" we attend.

Questions most asked of experiencers once on the Other Side are: Who did you help? Who did you serve?

How do you answer that? Name a few folks who are closest to you? Those you enjoy being around? A kindly neighbor? Passersby? The guy who robbed you? Grandma? Your kids? People you hate? Do questions like these really matter after you die? This love everybody stuff?

Seldom is there judgment. You face yourself with this one, with the "eyes" of your soul wide open. Yes, love matters, not just on this side but on the Other Side as well.

When you return from death or near-death a new commandment courses throughout your veins and in rhythm with your heartbeat . . . love one another. Experiencers of every stripe, tongue, culture, religion, and mindset find themselves beginning to behave in a manner as if life itself is all about love. In those countries that have no word or understanding of what we call "love," they find themselves becoming more compassionate, more understanding, more altruistic. We are either told during our episode to be more helpful to others or we naturally move in that direction, incorporating some form of self-less service into everyday life.

Born again. That's the phrase that applies. Not because of any religious dictim or faith-based ritual, but in the most *literal sense* born again. That second chance most believe they now have takes on the appearance of a second look—at a world very much worth living in.

Have you noticed? Invariably, experiencers are drawn to sustainable measures of every kind, organic gardening, diets brimming full of veggies with smaller portions of meats, earth-based architecture, geodesic domes, ecology, personalized and alternative medicines and healing measures, innovative design and creativity, better ways of doing business that incorporate the leadership potential of both females and males, education available to each child everywhere, bartering, fair tax laws, democratic debates and voting processes, accountability, churches as a fellowship of prayer and caring, the demise of religious intolerance and "the killing of infidels." The majority have no stomach for sexual exploitation or the excesses of greed, drugs, and power. The paycheck loses its grip as a motivator. Volunteerism takes its place.

The rediscovery of life's values enlivens experiencer voices: what needs fixing can be fixed, who needs loving can be loved. This translates to a keen sense of self-governance, self-motivation, and self-control. Cooperation defines how the average experiencer participates in group energy. Connectedness between people begins to override the need for shoving and pushing one's way up some proverbial "ladder."

Sounds great, doesn't it? Until you take a good look at the face in the mirror—yours. As experiencers begin to rethink, redo, relearn, and reassert themselves, mostly in new or different ways, a nagging question surfaces: why do I need a body? I'm a Divine Being, an Immortal Soul, we say. Yet, that face in the mirror demands equal time.

When I faced this question, I saw the self I was residing within a collective of all manner of organs, cells, tubular networks, bones, and blood—each microscopic piece intelligent and capable of memory and awareness. This collective formed the body I saw in the mirror, what I could feel and touch and comprehend, directed by a brain that operated like a circuit board. What fueled me was food, drink, air, thoughts, emotions. But what powered me was that Greater Breath that pulsed aliveness throughout the whole of creation, not just me.

In coming to grips with this simple understanding, life made sense. I could acknowledge my body as the living temple of the Living God, filled with beings—parts and pieces—cycling through births and deaths and rebirths as they, too, grew and evolved, all the myriad forms of intelligence, all the promise and the potential, all that was inside me . . . this my body, the incredible collective I wear. I came to see that it was a privilege, an incredible privilege, to have a body quite alive and be who I am where I am. Having love for others meant having love for myself—all of me.

Our various comings and goings during our lifespan are not accidental. One experiencer came back knowing he is here to save the world's tallest, strongest, oldest trees by cloning them. Another found a way to harness light in ways that can be used to increase bodily health and longevity. A woman woke up to her own incredibleness and when she did, she reached out to others, producing classes and seminars large and small that have helped thousands wake up too. A neurosurgeon discovered heaven and set the world "ablaze" with the passion of his excitement. The list of near-death experiencers who, once revived, go on to make changes large and small would fill hundreds of books.

Why are we here?

The question remains, irrespective of what we think is the answer.

Of the thousands I studied, about thirty percent or so returned convinced that reincarnation—life after life—is the only valid explanation for how our soul can correct any mistake it may have made in its own journeys. The majority still avoid such assumptions, preferring instead to think more in terms of the soul, each soul, as having a will of its own.

A situation I was involved in back in my home state of Idaho speaks to this type of scenario, that of a soul having a will beyond that of "personality." It involved two girls, best of friends, who were about to graduate from high school.

The year before, one of the girls calmly told her parents she would die in a violent accident the day before she graduated. This upset her parents. They sent her to several psychologists for evaluation but nothing was found to be amiss. No dream. No vision. She just knew. When the fateful day came, she and her best friend were sitting in a car at an intersection, waiting for the light to change. Suddenly, a car careened out of control and slammed head-on into theirs, killing both girls. Police discovered a note written by the daughter, revealing that she knew her best friend would be killed at the same time in the same accident as she would. Investigators also discovered that the best friend had acted in a manner suggestive of someone who knew death was coming, even though there was no reason for her to think this. A year later both mothers had a dream on the same night where their deceased daughter appeared and explained why the accident happened. This dream was so vivid neither mother could keep it to herself. One told a friend of mine who contacted me. Between us we arranged for the psychologist of the first mother to invite both sets of parents over so the separate dreams could be heard. What both dreams revealed, the reason for the girls' untimely death, was this: both girls had agreed before birth to participate in the horrible death event for the purpose of one helping the other work through a lingering fear of dying violently.

One soul helped another soul.

I offer this story to you because it accurately reflects how near-death experiencers tend to view the various reasons for birth and death, why we come and go as we do. They seem to recognize that sometimes another agenda holds sway besides personal notions.

I've often been close on the heels of unexpected deaths: first as a policeman's daughter; later when my former husband became a crop-duster pilot specializing in night jobs, flying barely inches above the ground in tree-lined fields; and whenever called to give healing prayer for those who were ill or about to die. If appropriate, I asked questions about the deceased and their behavior before they died: were there any changes? Over the years, a peculiar pattern emerged . . . people who died suddenly or accidentally, subconsciously communicated their "knowingness" about what was to happen through a specific pattern of behavorial clues:

Full Death
The Subconscious Pattern of Knowing When

- Usually about three months to three weeks before their deaths, individuals begin to change behavior normal for them

- Subtle at first, this behavioral change begins as a need to reassess affairs and life goals—a shift from material concerns toward philosophical ones.

- This is followed by a need to see everyone who means anything special to them. If visits are not possible, they begin writing letters or calling on the phone, maybe e-mail, Twitter, or Facebook.

- As time draws near, the people become more serious about straightening out their affairs and/or training or instructing a loved one or a friend to take over in their stead. This instruction can be quite specific, sometimes involving details such as what is owed and what is not; what insurance

policies exist and how to handle them; how possessions should be dispersed; and what goals, programs,
or projects are yet undone and how to finish them.
Financial matters seem quite important, as is the
management of personal and private affairs.

- There is a need, almost a compulsion, to reveal
secret feelings and deeper thoughts, to say what has
not been said, especially to loved ones. There is usually also a desire for one last "fling," maybe to visit
special places and do what is most enjoyed.

- The need to settle affairs and wind up life's details
can become so obsessive that it appears "spooky" or
weird to others. Many times, there's a need to talk
over the possibility of "what if I die," as if the individual had a dream or premonition. The person may
on occasion seem morbid or unusually serious.

- Usually, about twenty-four to thirty-six hours before
death, the individuals relax and are at peace. They
often appear "high" on something because of their
unusual alertness, confidence, and sense of joy. They
exude a peculiar strength and positive demeanor as
if they were now ready for something important to
happen. Many take on a "glow" about them.

I've noticed this pattern in people from the age of four
on up, regardless of any expressed beliefs or intelligence level.
I have also observed it in some people who were later mur-
dered. Certainly, not everyone displays advance knowledge
about their coming death, but all of those in my investigations
did. I rather suspect the reason some do and others don't has
more to do with the individual's sensitivity to inner promptings, than any real knowing.

Because of what I have seen and heard throughout my life, in my own experiences, and discovered during the three-decades-plus I have investigated and researched near-death states, I have come to accept as reality that each person has a "life plan." Any claim of an afterlife begs that we also consider the reality of a *before* life.

Research of the pre-birth existence (PBE) has now been accepted as legitimate inquiry. This growing field covers more than hypnotists specializing in past-life regressions or people who believe that life-after-life journeys help the soul grow and evolve. Physicians have unique ways of testing this idea. One is to see how aware a baby is. David B. Cheek, M.D., a retired obstetrician, wrote a paper on the evidence he collected that suggests that by the time a woman realizes she is pregnant, the embryo is already aware of her and her surroundings—indicating that awareness may begin at conception.

Near-death cases readily confront issues like abortion and missing twins. More often than not, the child who was lost appears healthy and whole in the mother's near-death episode, in essence to say "Hello, I didn't die, I'm still here." This brings comfort to some, regret for others. Every aspect of the human condition unwinds during a near-death experience and afterward. Nothing is left out, especially what death really is and what it feels like to die. Based on first-person commentaries from over 3,000 adult experiencers of near-death states, here is a summary of what they shared.

What Death Is

There is a step-up of energy at the moment of death, an increase in speed as if you are suddenly vibrating faster than before.

Using radio as an analogy, this speed-up is comparable to having lived all your life at a certain radio frequency when all of a sudden someone or something comes along and flips the dial. That flip shifts you to another, higher wavelength. The original frequency where you once existed is still there. It did not change.

Everything is still just the same as it was. Only *you* changed, only *you* speeded up to allow entry into the next radio frequency on the dial.

As is true with all radios and radio stations, there can be bleed-overs or distortions of transmission signals due to interference patterns. These can allow or force frequencies to coexist or commingle for indefinite periods of time. Normally, most shifts on the dial are fast and efficient; but, occasionally, one can run into interference, perhaps from a strong emotion, a sense of duty, or a need to fulfill a vow or keep a promise. This interference could allow coexistence of frequencies for a few seconds, days, or even years (perhaps explaining hauntings); but, sooner or later, eventually, every given vibrational frequency will seek out or be nudged to where it belongs.

You fit your particular spot on the dial by your speed of vibration. You cannot coexist forever where you do not belong. Who can say how many spots there are on the dial or how many frequencies there are to inhabit. No one knows. You shift frequencies in dying. You switch over to life on another wavelength. You are still a spot on the dial but you move up or down a notch or two.

You don't die when you die. You shift your consciousness and speed of vibration. That's all death is . . . a shift.

What It Feels Like To Die

Any pain to be suffered comes first. Instinctively you fight to live. That is automatic. It is inconceivable to the conscious mind that any other reality could possibly exist beside the earth-world of matter bounded by time and space. We are used to it. We have been trained since birth to live and thrive in it. We know ourselves to be ourselves by the external stimuli we receive. Life tells us who we are and we accept its telling. That, too, is automatic, and to be expected.

Your body goes limp. Your heart stops. No more air flows in or out. You lose sight, feeling, and movement—although the ability to hear goes last. Identity ceases. The "you" that you once were becomes only a memory. There is no pain at the moment of death. Only peaceful silence . . . calm . . . quiet. But you still exist.

It is easy not to breathe. In fact, it is easier, more comfortable, and infinitely more natural not to breathe than to breathe. The biggest surprise for most people in dying is to realize that dying does not end life. Whether darkness or light comes next, or some kind of event, be it positive, negative, or somewhere in-between, expected or unexpected, the biggest surprise of all is to realize you are still you. You can still think, you can still remember, you can still see, hear, move, reason, wonder, feel, question, and tell jokes—if you wish.

You are still alive, very much alive. Actually, you're more alive after death than at any time since you were last born. Only the way of all this is different; different because you no longer wear a dense body to filter and amplify the various sensations you had once regarded as the only valid indicators of what constitutes life. You had always been taught one has to wear a body to live.

If you expect to die when you die, you will be disappointed.

The only thing dying does is help you release, slough off, and discard the "jacket" you once wore (more commonly referred to as a body).

When you die you lose your body. That's all there is to it. Nothing else is lost. You are not your body. It is just something you wear for a while, because living in the earthplane is infinitely more meaningful and more involved if you are encased in its trappings and subject to its rules.

5

HEAVEN AND HELL

Yes, there is a hell and people go there.

I know the majority of those who die and return to life claim the exact opposite, and they are adamant in doing so. Only unconditional love resides on the Other Side of death, they say. Whatever "kinks" need to be worked out, whatever darkness or difficulty, the soul's redemption is assured. Not to worry. Forgiveness rules.

In order to make sense of the various claims experiencers make, we must look at everything. There's more beyond claims of pro and con. To find that "more," we need to dig deep.

For starters, know that one in seven of those I had sessions with reported hellish, frightening, or unpleasant near-death experiences. Other researchers state that these types of episodes are rare. Well, I guess that depends on what you consider rare. I honestly believe there are lots of them, but the people who have them won't say anything. Maybe what holds them back is a sense of regret or shame or embarrassment or confusion. I really don't know. I only know that during the eighties people were more open about this than they are now. In 1989, for instance, I encountered more experiencers of hellish states than I did heavenly.

I'll never forget the time when I was signing books at a mall located where the locals shop in the older part of Las Vegas. This guy came up to me—as thin as a rail and as scruff-hard as Nevada sand. He pointed a bony finger at me and yelled: "You tell 'em, lady. All these books about near-death experiences and all these TV shows with folks talking about heaven, always heaven. They don't know what they're talkin' about. You do." He went on to berate other experiencers for lying to the public by claiming that everyone went to heaven. He would have none of that. His "elsewhere place" on the Other Side of death was tinged with terror and he wanted everyone to be so advised.

Nurses too spoke of "other" types of near-death experiences, those that were anything but lovely, places where no one would want to go. When other researchers heard about what I kept finding, they advised that I pass on such stories to them so more professional measures could be applied in handling them. Didn't work. I finally asked several experiencers why they would not allow M.D.'s and Ph.D.'s to hear their story. "Don't trust 'em," was the main answer. Eventually, Nancy Evans Bush, an experiencer of a frightening scenario, wrote *Dancing Past the Dark* as a way to probe hellish cases. She emphasized in her book that there are many ways to interpret these episodes. Mystical and religious pathways have always addressed the dark side of human nature and how exploring that is a necessary component to spiritual maturity.

Among what I found with people who experienced disturbing scenarios is that most of them seemed to have deeply repressed guilt, fears, and sorrows, a few even expected to be punished after they died for the way they had lived. I did not notice a predominance of such cases with fundamentalists of any type of religion or belief system. Hell-fire and brimstone stories were few and far between. Descriptions of icy cold landscapes, abandonment, spinning vortexes, or having to face what they most feared—far outnumbered religious threats or medieval tortures.

Child experiencers, and those who had their experience as a child, were the ones who challenged me the most in this regard. I had to reconsider everything near-death experiencers of any age seemed to mean when they spoke of hell, or even heaven. Here's a couple of examples that really spun me around.

A woman vividly remembered dying nine days after her birth during surgery to remove an abscess from a severe staph infection. She had drawn pictures of what happened to her, over and over again, ever since she could hold a pencil. While I was with her she drew yet another one, depicting an oval operating table or perhaps a crib-like or incubator type affair with a bubble top. Overhanging was a large bright light fix-ture. White gowned figures, most of them women, stared at her. She also drew pictures of the follow-up treatments she endured from ray lamps. At first glance, one could conclude that her drawings simply showed how a typical surgical room, operating staff, equipment, and the kind of ongoing treat-ment one might expect, would look to a mere babe. But her recollection is of torture and being threatened by a deep-throated "Inner Stranger" who continued harassing her for years afterward. A deep sense of distrust resulted, until, in her early twenties, other-worldly guidance from a second near-ness with death explained the whys of the earlier one. A ques-tion to ask here is *how could a nine-day-old infant register so precisely such a scene and remember it lifelong?* Also, *what about that second sce-nario that healed the effects of the first one?*

A young man from New Zealand, with tears flooding his eyes, told me about a time, when he was barely seven, that he died of a high fever from pneumonia. He had disobeyed his parents about playing outside, overdoing it when he had not sufficiently recovered from a previous illness. Confined to bed, alone, frightened, and guilt-ridden, he left his painfully hot body and in an out-of-body state went in search of help. He described "walking" through the house and seeing his father enter through the front door. He ran to his father with arms outstretched, believing that help had been found. His father looked him in the face, then ran right past him, ignoring his pleas. The boy was invisible to his father, but he didn't know this at the time. He was heart-broken by what his father did and decided that, because of this, he wasn't good enough to be loved anymore. He never saw how panic-stricken his father was once the boy's lifeless body was discovered, nor the heroic efforts his father made to save him. When he revived in the hospital, all he remembered was pleading for help and being refused. He withdrew from his family after that and remained estranged from his father for many years. No amount of counseling made any difference until we spoke, and he could finally understand what had happened to him as a youngster and why.

Both of these experiencers as children were horrified by what happened to them and that horror extended into adulthood. What the young mostly go through, like with these two, is hardly the stuff of dungeon lore, still, some of their drawings do depict scary monsters, hurtful scenes, stern judges, and even the devil himself. Adult episodes of this type are no different. Irrespective of horrors heaped upon an experiencer, the awful stuff can be interpreted as somehow instructive, or perhaps a "message" that needs to be noticed, or maybe revealed testimony from the spirit world.

What happened at a packed hall after a talk I gave put the whole issue of heaven and hell into a new and different

perspective for me—and—I hope for you, too. I had asked
for volunteers to come up, anyone who had yet to reveal what
had happened to him or her at death's edge. Two accepted the
invitation. The first was a man, probably in his early-thirties,
who described one of the most beautiful heavenly-type episodes I had ever heard. Absolutely wondrous. Hardly a dry-
eye in the place when he finished. Then he shocked the entire
audience by saying this was the worst thing that had ever happened to him. He felt cursed and regretted the whole affair,
and wished the changes it brought about in his life would go
away. A woman a little older than he jumped up. She described
a scenario of darkness and thunder and piercing wind, and how
she had to fight to save herself from being sucked downward
into a bottomless whirlpool. Exhausted, she managed to grab
at the shore and pull herself out of the water. Her wrap-up was
another shocker when she said this was the best thing that ever
happened to her. She considered the experience proof positive that she could handle any obstacle: she could survive any
threat. The woman was glowing and animated as she spoke.

The heavenly experience was viewed as a curse. The hellish one, a special gift. This one event effectively demonstrates
that any sense of judgment as to whether a given experience
was positive or negative, or took place in heaven or hell, is a
mistake. *Only the experiencer can decide.*

You go where you fit when you die. I'm talking energy
here because we are energy beings. We vibrate. Everything
does. The scenarios of near-death states show that once you—
the real you—leave your body in death, you eventually find
yourself moving to or present within a vibratory frequency
you energetically resonate with. What you find within that
frequency corresponds to what you are capable of responding
to (i.e., types of beings, shapes, forms, activities, landscapes).

These frequency realms resemble a "layer cake" of many levels, each separated from the other by degrees of lighter, finer vibrations or heavier, denser ones.

To understand what I'm saying, hang out with experiencers as I have. Snuggle up and absorb their words, feelings, their sense of awe tinged with the fear of too much, too simple, too perfect. It's as if the symbols of their culture, their religion, and their dreams fail utterly in comparison with the real thing . . . *the real afterlife of heaven, hell, the borderlands (an in-between where some souls roam around, appear to be lost, or simply wait), and judgment.*

A summary statement follows of what I culled from more than three decades of doing this work.

The Truth About Hell

The heavier, more dense vibrations hold what most people call "hell" because these are the frequencies where difficult, hurtful, or lower forms of thought reside, and in close proximity to the earthplane. This is where we go to work out whatever blocks us from the power of our own light: hang-ups, addictions, fears, guilt, anger, rage, regrets, self-pity, arrogance, resentments. We stay in hell (and there are many divisions of this vibratory frequency) for however long best serves our development. We do not leave until we have changed our attitudes, thoughts, and feelings, and are ready for another opportunity to improve and advance.

The Truth About Heaven

The faster, higher, more subtle vibratory frequencies are what most people term "heaven," and they also are fairly close to the earthplane. We go there to recognize or enjoy whatever reveals the power of our own light: talents, abilities, joys, courage, generosity, caring, empathy, virtue, diligence, patience, thoughtfulness, and loving kindness. There is a sense of benefit here, as if one has found one's true home. We stay in heaven (and there are many levels here, too) for however long it takes to experience the glory of love and the power of forgiveness. We leave whatever level of this helpful, supportive domain we are in once we have further advanced as an awakened soul and are more unified in spirit.

I counted what appeared to be twelve heavens and twelve hells from experiencer descriptions. Yet, this "layer cake" of vibratory frequencies (levels or realms we can inhabit) appears to be open at both ends. I found nothing to indicate or suggest otherwise. Claims that souls can be forever and eternally trapped or condemned in the heavier vibratory levels, or bask in the glory of ascension in the finer, lighter ones, do not hold up. When you study what experiencers encounter on the other side of death as I have, you come to recognize the power unleashed once the individual revives and he or she begins to understand what just happened. To whatever degree he or she is affected, the soul responds. Consciousness expands when this occurs . . . personally and collectively.

Borderlands

"Detours" happen—to places like borderlands or shadow areas where individuals in spirit form may tarry. In some cases the ego personality refuses to fully merge with its soul, remaining instead "apart" or "earthbound." This situation can be temporary or long-lasting. The cause for this seems generally to be either the intensity of the individual's desire to remain embodied, or perhaps because of disorientation, confusion, feeling lost, or maybe still linked to a vow or a promise the individual is determined to fulfill. Catchall places in the borderlands appear to be necessary diversions so that one can shake free of that which initially hinders. Many religions and spiritual traditions make allowance for such "death distress" by encouraging the living to pray for the departed, so any who are lost may be found.

The Truth About Judgment

The presence of a judge who determines who goes to heaven or hell does occur in some near-death narratives, mostly in cases throughout Asia, Africa, and amongst native peoples regardless of culture. As strange as it may seem, it's the kids—anywhere in the world—who most often have judgment-type scenarios. These usually consist of the child being met by a "critical or caring" parent-type-figure who "fetches them up:" scolds or encourages, teaches or warns, to prepare them for their future. Children sometimes face tribunals, usually with animal judges. Occasionally, a child will talk about animal heaven, where they had to go before they could visit the heaven where people are.

The notion that religious tenets determine where people go once dead, does not match testimonials from the vast majority of experiencer accounts. Something else appears to be the prime mover . . . self-acceptance or self-rejection. You may be a doer of great deeds, pay out millions to help the needy, but inside be an empty mess. Or, you may be nothing more than a petty thief with a string of failures, but you really tried and you kept on trying to pull yourself up. What we really are inside our deepest self creates our energetic signal or "imprint." This imprint has more to do with where we go after dying than any judge or tribunal or religious edict.

Summary aside, the "layer cake" of numerous levels, and I've seen them too, appears to me as if some type of "construct" or open-ended system, powered by choice, that enables us to move from level to level, realm to realm. On the other side of death, we remain wherever we find ourselves only for as long as we believe we can or feel we must. Nothing is static. When I caught on to this, how things appear to really operate, I was overwhelmed by the fairness of it. If ever there was proof of a Higher Intelligence/A Loving God, this is it. Such a simple yet incredibly elegant design transcends human expectation.

What puzzles me, though, is the virtual absence of religious comment about an afterlife, heaven or hell, borderlands, judgment, or even the existence of a soul and how we might progress as souls in today's world. Those pastors, ministers, and clerics who do bring up the subject of an afterlife tread carefully, insisting that only exclusivity wins, that only their parishioners will ascend to heaven's heights.

Clearly this is not so. Near-death experiencers across the world—people of any age, race, culture, religion, or mindset—undergo this phenomenon and return to life awakened to the transcendent reality of God/Allah/Deity, souls, and a pattern of aftereffects that lead in most cases to physiological and psychological changes—a real and certain newness.

Fact: the near-death experience validates what the world's great religions teach. Except for one thing: underscored by the phenomenon is that God is the God of all. Religions teach us how to live, give us instructions, encouragement, hope, inspiration, upliftment, and a helping hand when we need it—from cradle to grave. None of them own the Deity they worship. No prophet, rabbi, minister, pope, guru, cleric, imam, master teacher, shaman, medium, psychic, pastor, or leader of any spiritual, mystical, or religious group, can determine what will happen when one dies. That vibratory imprint, that resonance factor of what we have become—who we really are inside the heart and soul of us—determines what comes next.

A sad fact: those religious leaders who talk about near-death experiences from the pulpit can be and sometimes are scolded or fired for doing so.

A happy fact: nothing is shutting them up.

The near-death experience is slowly becoming part of religious discourse; not as a threat, but as a consistent, modern-day revelation of the true power of love and forgiveness . . . what every religion has taught since its inception.

6

NEAR-DEATH EXPERIENCES

An older definition of the phenomenon, created by the International Association for Near-Death Studies, has yet to be topped. I offer it to you now.

> *The near-death experience is an intense awareness, sense, or experience of otherworldliness, whether pleasant or unpleasant, that happens to people who are at the edge of death. It is of such magnitude that most experiencers are deeply affected, many to the point of making significant changes in their lives because of what happened to them. Aftereffects often last lifelong and can intensify over time.*

Most of you are familiar with the work of Raymond E. Moody, Jr., M.D., Ph.D., and his list of components and aspects that came to comprise what is now called "near-death experiences"—ineffability (beyond the limits of any language to describe); hearing yourself pronounced dead; feelings of peace and quiet; hearing unusual noises; seeing a dark tunnel; finding yourself outside your body; meeting "spiritual beings;" a very bright light experienced as a "being of light;" a panoramic life review; sensing a border or limit to where you can go; coming back into your body; frustrating attempts to tell others about what happened to you; subtle "broadening and deepening" of your life afterward; elimination of the fear of death; corroboration of events witnessed while out of your body. He later added: a realm where all knowledge exists; cities of light; a realm of bewildered spirits; and supernatural rescues.

Keep in mind that I never heard any of this during the initial phase of my work. Because scenarios and the components in them are as individual as the people who have them—you guessed it—what I found differed from the accepted version. The job I had then required constant travel throughout Central, Northern, and Southern states. This enabled me to meet folks, usually at construction, business, and military sites, yet also at truck stops, hospitals, schools, churches, hotel/motel complexes, on elevators, at taxi stands and airports.

Of the stories the people told me, four components stood out as the most commonly reported. Primary were vivid, detailed out-of-body experiences with 360-degree vision. Many could prove details because of testimony offered from nurses, friends, even strangers. Second was that light, brighter than bright, a light that knows you and can converse with you. The power of this light was described as "massive." As part of the death or near-death event, "visitors" often manifested, sometimes to chat but mostly in the role of "spirit guide." Pre-deceased relatives and pets were the most frequently reported, yet friends appeared as greeters, too, or maybe a light being, angel, or religious figure.

Life reviews were fairly common and usually centered around a brief backward glance to see what was gained or lost in life. A tribunal could be there to pass judgment, or scenes of one's life simply passed by or were relived in a detached manner. Some experiencers, though, underwent a more radical type of review where they had to *face and feel* whatever harm they did to another. This type of review was painful. Seldom did a child have the radical kind, but a few did.

Missing, as a major component were tunnels. Not that many people ever reported them, and still do not. In fact, Gallup Poll in their 1982 scientific survey of near-death experiencers pegged only nine percent. The rise in tunnel reports began after the media sensationalized Moody's *Life After Life*. Thanks to what happened, the public lexicon gained a new word used to describe any form of darkness or unusual movements in darkness toward light. Near-death experiences are ineffable. Remember? How do you or anyone else describe something that cannot be named? We needed a word. Moody fashioned one.

Of the thousands of stories I've heard, the various scenarios are consistent in how they seem to fit into this type of patterning.

- *Brief (initial) experiences* involve maybe one or two elements, possibly three—such as a loving nothingness, the living dark, a friendly voice, brief out-of-body experience, or just a greeter. No life reviews with this type. (My research, based on 3,000 experiencers: 76 percent of the children had this, 20 percent with adults.)

- *Unpleasant (distressing) experiences, maybe hellish*, include such things as encounters with a threatening void, stark limbo, or hellish purgatory, or scenes of a startling and unexpected indifference (like being shunned), even hauntings from one's own past, or having to face "unfinished business." Life reviews are common. (Three percent with children, 15 percent with adults.)

- *Pleasant (radiant) experiences, perhaps heavenly,* often center around scenarios of loving family reunions with those who have previously died, reassuring religious figures or light beings, validation that life counts, affirmative and inspiring dialogue, lovely landscapes. Life reviews common. Some have life previews. (Nineteen percent with children, 47 percent with adults.)

- *A more collective (transcendent) experience,* confronts scenes beyond personal frames of reference; sometimes shown historical truths, other-worldly dimensions, given a tour of the universe, or instructed about greater and more enduring wisdoms. Life reviews are rare. Collective previews common—about the world's future, evolutionary changes, creation itself. (Two percent with children, 18 percent with adults.)

Sprinkled throughout types of patterning is a broad range of additional components that are occasionally reported, things like: heavenly colleges, sparkling cities, fields of grass that glitter from their own inner light, flowers that talk, dancers, music unlike that of earth, walks with Jesus or other religious figures, family secrets revealed, the unknown unveiled—including the legendary Book of Life in which all things are said to be recorded.

As I previously warned, never affix "positive" or "negative" to any of this.

You fall into the trap of judgment if you do. Be alert if any experiencer comes back saying, "I was chosen" or, "Listen to me I was shown the real truth" or, "Nothing will ever happen to you when you die that will hurt." Even though revelations may vary from one experiencer to another, overall, episodes are startlingly similar anywhere in the world. Differences that show up depend more on the language constraints and cultural tendencies of the experiencer, than on fabrication. With the young, it depends on what they were exposed to since seven months en utero. I say this because one-third of the child experiencers I had sessions with could remember being in the womb, and their memories began around seven months en utero. Most of what they told me was verified by mothers or other close family members. Because of this, I can say: *children by nature can remember birth and pre-birth events—especially if strong emotions were expressed.*

Toss any connection you think might exist to topics like parapsychology, paranormal, super-conscious, psychic talents, wishful thinking, visionary dreams, New Age meanderings, or imagination gone wild. Near-death experiences are not related to nor an outgrowth from any such categories.

Average length of time without vital signs is from five to twenty minutes. Notice I said "average." Some "wake up" in the morgue—much to the shock of morgue personnel.

Since the brain must have oxygen within three to four minutes or brain damage can occur, a signature feature of near-death states is: *although some do show retardation to a degree after reviving or being resuscitated, the vast majority return smarter than before—as if brain enhanced—literally, intelligence improves.* This is especially noticeable with children who had their experience before age six, and doubly-true with babes who seem to have died or nearly died in the womb, during birth, or up to fifteen months of age. A frontispiece in my book, *The New Children and Near-Death Experiences*, was written by John Raymond Liona, who remembers having had his near-death episode inside his mother's vagina while he was being born (the cord tightly coiled around his neck). "The Riddle of Consciousness," a

report about an experiment that looked objectively at the rudi-
ments of infant consciousness, was published in the May 2013
issue of *Science*. The discovery? Babies between five and fifteen
months exhibit "a biological signature of consciousness." That
means, new babes by their very nature are consciously aware
of the world around them, with brains engaged. This finding
sheds more light on what I found, and may explain why a tiny
one's near-death experience is almost always remembered as
if the child now possessed a state of consciousness higher than
what their age suggests.

If you think children's cases are utterly amazing, check
this out about adults.

Pim van Lommel, M.D., director of a large study done
of heart patients in The Netherlands (*Lancet Medical Journal*,
12-15-01), makes this extraordinary assessment:

> *When an individual is without vital signs (no breath, no pulse, no
> brain waves), an individual can still have detailed and vivid out-of-
> body experiences, clear enhanced consciousness, self-identity with
> emotions, cognition—thought perception, full use of faculties, and
> intact memories.*

Further verification of his assessment comes from resuscitation expert, Sam Parnia, M.D., in an interview he had
with Brandon Keim on April 24, 2013, for *Wired Science*:

> *"When you die, there's no blood flow going into your brain. If it goes
> below a certain level, you can't have electrical activity. It takes a lot
> of imagination to think there's somehow a hidden area of your brain
> that comes into action when everything else isn't working . . . The
> historical idea is that electrochemical processes in the brain lead*

to consciousness. That may no longer be correct, because we can
demonstrate that those processes don't go on after death."

Skeptics piecemeal the experience, saying that a certain
aspect is caused by one thing while another aspect is caused
by something else. Pieces. Then there's the group who think
they've proved that all out-of-body experiences happen in the
brain. Yet all they established is that the "doppelganger effect"
is real (that phantom images of self can be created at will).
Any good shaman knows this. How about the claim that near-
death experiences are some type of epilepsy (brain misfires),
when we already know that the images and feelings from such
seizures are superficial and totally lack the pattern of near-
death aftereffects. Then there's "proof" that near-death states
are simply a brain-wave abnormality, maybe a higher rate of
sleep disorder. The control group for this study consisted of
colleagues and friends of the experimenter, only four yes or
no questions were used, no previous workup or testing was
done, and [get this] the experimenters completely ignored the
fact that their subjects only gained the new brain-wave patterns *after* their near-death episode. The point of their study
fizzled. Same thing with the God Spot in the Sylvan Fissure
of the brain as the location of such experiences (theory based
only on one case, very sketchy, most scenario aspects missing);
and the God Helmut (only fragmentary imagery, no scenario
patterning, no lifelong aftereffects).

I could go on and on like this but I would only bore you.

There is not a single skeptic you can name who has done
a study of any appreciable size of both adult and child near-
death experiencers, who focused on types/elements/scenar-
ios, took into account the broad range of death conditions
plus the lifelong pattern of physiological and psychological

aftereffects, and then checked what could be verified with significant others. Skeptics do piecemeal, taking one or a few things out of context from the whole. This is conjecture and proves nothing.

Near-death experiences are realer than real.

Hallucinations? Oxygen deprivation? Drug effects? Hypercarbia? Visual deception? Products of a dying brain? If you believe any of this piecemeal "science," then explain the following episodes (all of them investigated and verified).

A YOUNG WOMAN CRITICALLY injured in a car/truck accident, rushed to the hospital by medics, died during surgery but was successfully resuscitated. While still on the operating table, she opened her eyes and in a very animated manner began to speak of seeing her Dad. He told her he had just died, how and why he did, and that his time had come. He also said she couldn't stay dead because she had things yet to accomplish in her life before she could fulfill her life plan. Her animated testimony became a problem for the surgeons as she wouldn't hold still, nor would she quit talking about her Dad. One of them went to the waiting room where some of her family had gathered to discuss the situation. Family members assured the doctor that she must be hallucinating as the father was in excellent health, one of them had spoken to him on the phone that very morning. When the physician told her this, she became even more excited, her face began to glow. Almost angry, the doctor returned to the gathered family and insisted that they get the father on the phone right that very minute. *Suffice it to say, numerous phone calls later, the family discovered that the father had died five minutes before the daughter did and exactly in the same manner she had described.*

A MAN IN PORTLAND, OREGON was out driving north of town around midnight, the dark of the moon, late October. A sudden temperature drop created black ice on the roadway of tight switch-backs. Driving much too fast, he missed one, crashed head-on into a large tree. He said he floated up to the top of the tree, looked down, saw his car in pieces, blood everywhere, and his right arm gone. His choice was to save his body. No dwellings were close, but he spied one on a hill nearby, saw a light coming from a window on the second floor. He described floating over to that window and, seeing a man inside, jumped up and down and screamed at the man: "There's been an accident. Call the police." The guy inside later told the police:

"There was this jumping fog outside my window. Fog doesn't jump up and down. I just stared at that fog and then heard a loud voice in my ear yelling, "There's been an accident. Call the police.' I did, then I grabbed a flashlight and went downstairs and outside. Took me a while to find the wreck."

Physicians saved the man but couldn't save his arm. He had been a right-handed, professional artist who now had to also deal with blindness caused by force of impact. Two months later his sight returned. He requested pencil and paper, and with his left hand drew a picture of the accident scene, every single minute detail. *The guy in the house and the investigating police officers were called and asked to study the drawing. All were stunned. There was no way the man could have seen anything that night, yet his drawing was so accurate it was as if a photograph of the accident scene.*

A FETUS ALMOST FULL-TERM remembers angry voices, male and female, a sense of alarm, something drastically not as it should be, male accusing female of killing his son. Two weeks previously, the doctor had informed the pregnant mother that there was no heartbeat, the baby was dead. What the unborn heard was her drunken father screaming in rage as he grabbed her mother and sent her flying across the room, right into the corner of a large table which ruptured her amniotic sac. The mother was rushed to the hospital, where a "dead baby girl" was delivered via an emergency cesarean section. The hairy heap no one had paid attention to began to breathe. The attending physician warned the parents that the baby could not possibly survive, thus he was able to obtain permission from them to try thirty-one experimental procedures on the infant. Named Carroll, she remembers looking at "the baby" in the glass thing three days later and determining that its heart and lungs were working but not its stomach. "Little lashes. Eyes moving under thin lids. Not my face. After all, it's a baby and I'm not. It might just make it. Is that good or bad?" The attending physician (who happened to be the drinking buddy of the father, that's why the assault was never reported) noted bad nights followed by rallies—nothing hopeful—but against all odds, the child lived. *At the age of two and a half and at a family gathering, in front of both parents, Carroll repeated back to her father every word he had said when he threw her mother into the table. She also described the situation and furniture placement. Her parents were dumbfounded. No one knew the full story of what had occurred, nor had the parents discussed it between themselves.*

IN 1976, A VOCAL communist dissident in Tbilisi, Georgia (then part of Russia) by the name of George Rodonaia was run over twice by a car driven by a member of the KGB, as he was waiting for a taxi to take him to the airport. Rushed to the hospital, pronounced dead, his body was shoved into a morgue freezer vault. After three days his body was wheeled over to autopsy where a team of doctors commenced splitting open his lower torso. His eyes opened. One doctor thinking this a mere reflex, closed his eyes and continued cutting. This happened again, and once again no one thought anything of it. The third time his eyes popped open, the doctor jumped backward, screamed, and had to take a one-month leave of absence.

Rodonaia's own uncle was one of the attending physicians. Many surgeries later, an unbelievable story emerged of what happened to him after he died, what he saw, and what he did during those three days he was supposedly a corpse. His narrative is a long one—of visiting Paris and trying to talk with people who heard but could not see him, of going back in time to witness the execution of both parents by the KGB (he was raised by an aunt and uncle who never discussed the fate of his parents), of entering into the minds of his friends to see if they really were friends, and of discovering that the pregnant wife of one of them had delivered. Instantly he confronted the crying baby, scanned her as if possessed of X-ray vision, spied a broken hip, and "knew" the head nurse had dropped her. He was also inside his wife's head when she picked his gravesite, and, at the same time, made mental lists of eligible bachelors, pros and cons. She was now a widow and had two kids to think about. Rodonaia never wrote a book about his experience, but his wife verified that . . . it took three days for the swelling of his tongue to recede so he could talk. His first words were about the baby. Rodonaia was a physician himself. He detailed the exact break of the child's hip to doctors and then told them about the head nurse. She confessed when confronted and was fired. The "lists" his wife had made in her head while standing at the grave, each man, each trait, he recounted accurately. This so shocked and frightened her that she would have nothing to do with him for a year. "Why," I asked. Her reply: "I had no privacy. We had to learn how to live together again."

RUSHED TO THE HOSPITAL with severe phlebitis, Margaret Fields Kean died on the operating table. A colorful, lovely world opened up for her during her near-death episode where only peace and unconditional love existed. She sensed she had a choice to make while there. Her only thought was, "Where could I best be of service?" Her answer: becoming a healer, once back inside her human body, seemed best. Instantly she knew everything, including why she had a daughter and that it was important that she live to finish raising her. A Light came. She knew the Light was God so she anchored that Light in her spirit and soul and accepted her mission of healing. After being resuscitated and while still in the recovery room, she became aware of a young man nearby in great pain. She spoke softly to him and soothed him to sleep. She then "projected" into the shuttered isolation room of a white boy charred black by severe burns. She sat on his bed, introduced herself by name, and counseled him about his purpose in life. She told him it was okay if he chose to die, for God was loving, and he had nothing to fear. Months later, while continuing her recovery as an out-patient and still in pain, Fields Kean was attending a horse show when a couple, hearing the loudspeaker announce her daughter's name as a winner, sought her out. They were the parents of the severely burned boy. Before he had died, he told them about his meeting with her and relayed all the wonderful truths she had told him about God and about life. The parents were thrilled to have finally located her, so they could personally say thanks for what she had done for their son. *The dying boy had identified her by name, even though the two had never physically seen each other or verbally spoken in any manner, nor had any nurse known that the two had ever communicated, nor had it ever been possible that she could have known if the isolation room was even occupied when she "projected" into it.* Fields Kean went on to discover what health really is and launched a drive to learn all she could about nutrition and organic gardening. It took her years to discover what would heal her incessant leg pain. Once she did, she became a healer and developed what came to be called "The Results System," a technique that enables anyone to access the wisdom of "inner knowing."

She eventually moved to South Africa and worked with the sangomas (native healers) of Swaziland and Transkei.

These cases transcend medical and scientific models of what might have occurred or how.

Now, allow me to stretch this whole subject even further. The *"near-death-like" experience* mimics everything I've just said—everything—except that the people who have it are either scared they might die (a fear death), could have died but didn't (a close-call), or were in perfect health with no apparent problems (a real puzzle). Examples follow.

- On a Sunday morning, a woman was bent over picking up a large newspaper dropped on her porch. She straightened, looked into the rising sun, seemed somehow to enter the sun, and had a full-blown near-death experience followed by the full pattern of physiological and psychological aftereffects that engender lifelong changes.

- A man walking across his living room to adjust the window turned to walk back to his sofa when the room suddenly filled with light. He physically and completely conscious walked straight into a lengthy near-death scenario that enabled him to better understand the Bible. Aftereffects were unending, as was his passion to "spread the good news" about biblical text.

- A near-death experiencer who had an incredible episode and revived in a morgue—went on to have a near-death-like experience 17 years later while delivering the eulogy for a friend recently killed.

This event was far more powerful than the previous encounter, transforming her in ways beyond imagining.

These three episodes are not typical spiritual or "mountain-top" experiences that awaken an individual to the existence of other-worldly realities. They are breakthrough events that led to total or near-total transformations of consciousness. Because so many of this type of episode are now reported, a separate category had to be created to include them in with the study of near-death experiences; hence the term "near-death-like experience."

As long as we're talking about "exceptions to the rule" that aren't really exceptions after all, I'd like to mention a few more.

- *Conception*—there are a number of near-death cases where individuals as part of their episode found that they were present, when, at conception, they could pick the genes they felt they needed—hair, face, body features, and whether or not they would be handicapped and in what manner.

- *Handicapped*—many are those who were shown why. The number one reason given for the handicap? "I'm here to teach people about love." From one experiencer: "The specific choice of cystic fibrosis was to help me learn dignity in suffering. My understanding in the eternal sense was complete—I knew that I was a powerful, spiritual being that chose to have a short, but marvelous, mortal existence."

- *Birth*—both child and adult experiencers tell stories about being met on the other side of death by those who were aborted, missing twins (where one mysteriously died before birth or was reabsorbed back into the womb), and genetic parents who were previously unknown to them and who had passed on long before.

Survivors of clinical death, near-death, and near-death-like experiences challenge every detail of what we call life, every nuance of what we believe is true, especially in regards to the unborn. Narratives vary. Overall, though, the most repeated phrase spoken by near-death experiencers afterward is: *always there is life.*

Stop a minute.

Take another look at those four words.

They literally mean there is *no before life, no now life, no afterlife.* They mean . . . always on some level in some form in some place or dimension or realm there is life. We have always existed. We exist now. We will always exist. Eternity is our home. We never left where we began. Only the scenery changed when eternity pretended to be time.

Steve Jobs is quoted as saying:

> *Remembering that I'll be dead soon is the most important tool I've ever encountered to help me make the big choices in life. Because all external expectations, all pride, all fear of embarrassment or failure just fall away in the face of death, leaving only what is truly important. Remembering you are going to die is the best way I know to stop thinking you have something to lose. You are already naked. There is no reason not to follow your heart.*

His last words as he lay dying, seemingly gazing through and past the loved ones present, were: "Oh wow, oh wow, oh wow!"

7

NEAR-DEATH AFTEREFFECTS

May I have your attention, please?

A correction is due.

Regardless of what you believe or have been told, the near-death experience is *not* just a light show with predominant features and/or a storyline. It is an extraordinary phenomenon that consists of an other-worldly episode PLUS a pattern of physiological and psychological aftereffects that affect one physically, mentally, emotionally, and spiritually . . . over extended periods of time . . . with most, lifelong.

Did you get that?

Experience. Aftereffects. One phenomenon—with two distinct parts.

Now that we've cleared up this misunderstanding, follow me as we explore the other half of the phenomenon, and we begin by admitting returning to life after a near-death experience is a shock.

The world around us that we all grew up in and continue to live in and are committed to as "the only game in town," this dependable reality that is solid and real, appears gray afterward. Like, where we were, a stereo-phonic, wraparound, digitally enhanced, super chromatic, 360-degree instantaneous splash of colors and sites and sounds and movements we don't even have on earth . . . hello? . . How do you compare there with here? You can't. Depression can set in. You feel as if you were kicked out of heaven, and for what? Life back here? Some bargain. There are those who attempt suicide to get back on the Other Side. Some succeed. Most stay, and gladly, because they know they are here for a reason and they want to get on with it. They may miss where they once were, but their job is here.

Near-death experiences are both personal and collective. Although experiencers are the subject at hand (their lives and what they did about them afterward), what applies to the one applies to the many. The world is connected by more than just an Internet. Physicists have repeatedly demonstrated that everything on the quantum level is connected to everything else. Where that statement takes the phenomenon of near-death is straight toward the aftereffects—*the pattern of aftereffects is what verifies the experience*, not the other way around.

You cannot speak about near-death states without giving equal time to what comes next. And I'm not just talking about people losing their fear of death and becoming more spiritual and loving. The phenomenon has two sides, like a coin. To consider one side without the other breeds pop quizzes and superficiality.

For everyone's sanity, let's establish a broader context to the phenomenon by acknowledging that some people get the "light show" at death's edge while the larger number do not. Conservative estimates of those who do: 12 to 21 percent in the crisis/hospital environment, 4 to 5 percent general population worldwide.

Stress plays a role in who does and does not. That indicates there is a "before." I noticed stressors, conditions in the experiencer's life that point to either unrest or inattention. This type of condition was present in all the cases I have seen or been involved with. What caught my eye right along were episodes that occurred under circumstances such as: major life junctures when a decision needed to be made; times of deep dissatisfaction, disappointment, frustration; when feeling hurried all the time or excessively strained; while running a "tight ship," insisting on personal control; as one's ability to afford lifestyle maintenance toppled; excessively pushing limits—at work, at play, in everything; when demanding and strict rules limit one's beliefs and activities; when in strong denial or without meaningful goals; during "happy" times that were really a façade; when overly satisfied or complacent.

The common thread in each case is stress, lots of it. Even with babies and the unborn. Mother's stress, as well as that of the father, can readily become the child's stress. Sometimes it's as if the child has the experience for the parents or the doctors or for significant others . . . to relieve or heighten *their* stress. And the stress I refer to is the kind that narrows your focus so much that you become as if blind to the "bedrock" of your life—what's really true as opposed to what you think is or might be true. Shamans, spiritual and mystical folk, have for aeons of time referred to this type of stress as "high stress," and they fashioned certain rituals and practices that would "push" the probationer over the fear threshold in an act of facing the ultimate . . . so the ego would die and the true self could be born.

Indicators of high stress match the upshot of near-death cases. So does the reason most often given by the experiencers themselves to explain what they went through: "I got what I needed." Knowing this, the pattern I found of physiological and psychological aftereffects takes on greater meaning.

Physiological Aftereffects

Physiological aftereffects center mainly around changes in brain structure and function, the nervous and digestive systems, and skin sensitivity. Specifics include light and sound sensitivity, looking and acting younger with adults (the opposite with children), substantial changes in energy levels (can have energy surges), changes in thought processing (can switch from sequential/selective thinking to clustered abstracting with an acceptance of ambiguity), indications of brain structure/function changes, insatiable curiosity, lower blood pressure, brighter skin and eyes, reversal of brain hemisphere dominance with most, healing quicker, reversal of body clock with many, heightened intelligence, metabolic changes (doesn't take as long to process food, bowel movements can increase), assimilating substances into the bloodstream quicker (takes less for full effect), loss of tolerance for pharmaceuticals (most turn to alternative/-complementary healing measures), heightened response to taste-touch-texture-smell-pressure, more creative and inventive, increased allergies, electrical sensitivity, some display synesthesia (conjoined senses).

Psychological Aftereffects

Psychological aftereffects tend to merge compassion and creativity with enhancements of faculties normal to us. Specifics cover the loss of the fear of death, becoming more spiritual and less religious, more generous and charitable, handling stress easier, philosophical, more open and accepting of the new and different, disregard for time and schedules, regarding things as new even when they are not (boredom levels decrease), forming expansive concepts of love while at the same time challenged to initiate and maintain satisfying relationships, becoming psychic/intuitive, knowing things, can go through periods of depression, less competitive, having vivid dreams and visions, "inner child" issues exaggerate, convinced of life purpose and mission, rejection of previous limitations and norms, episodes of future knowing/future memory, more detached and objective (dissociation), "merge" easily (absorption), hunger for knowledge, challenged with communication, synchronicity commonplace, more orgasmic, healing ability, aware of invisible energy fields and auras, preference for open doors/open windows/open shades, drawn to nature and crystals, laughing more, exhibiting compassionate understanding.

A further look at how this stacks up percentage-wise with experiencers:

- *21 percent* claimed no discernible differences afterward (this claim was countered by the experiencer's significant others in numerous cases where I was able to obtain additional input).

- *60 percent* reported significant, noticeable changes.

- *19 percent* said changes were so radical they felt as if they had become another person (before and after photographs differed somewhat, although basic body type and facial structures remained the same).

- *79 percent* reported noticeable or significant changes after their near-death episode, exhibiting all or most of the pattern of aftereffects.

There is *no* drug (legal or illegal, natural or synthetic), no hallucination, no case of oxygen deprivation, no epileptic seizures . . . nothing that can match this pattern of aftereffects (except a deeply impactful transformation of consciousness).

The key with near-death research is to investigate the *entire* phenomenon, not just a few of its aspects. If you separate parts from the whole, you lose sight of the overall effect and meaning of the experience.

So, let's do it. Let's put everything in one basket and make that basket intimately personal . . . what the average near-death experiencer is like after such a shift:

- sensitive to light and sound, comfortable with silence

- highly intuitive, know things, seem guided

- comfortable with an awareness of things future

- wakes up around 3:00 to 4:00 a.m., vivid dreams

- prefers open windows, doors, closets, shades

- acutely aware of injustice, willing to make a difference

- animals and birds attracted to them

- has dilemmas with money and telling time

- challenged by contracts, rules, regulations—the idea of limits

- ecumenical—one family, one people, One God

- becomes an electrical sensitive—to some or greater degrees

- sensitive to pharmaceuticals, caution with child experiencers

- changes eating habits, blood pressure lowers

- more allergies, sensitive to smells and pressure changes

- can slip into depression and anger, recover quickly

- uses language differently, communication changes, new ideas

- smarter, more curious, hunger to learn

- affinity for nature, ecology, simplicity, spirits

- more loving, yet challenged to form lasting relationships

Did you notice that part about waking up around 3:00 a.m.? A curious finding until you start digging around.

Levels of melatonin (the hormone that regulates sleep) peak in the brain's pineal gland between 3 to 4:00 a.m., effectively converting light waves into energy. At the same time, the deeper function of the pineal gland goes into high gear producing DMT (N,N-dimethyltryptamine), considered the "spirit molecule" and associated with mystical experiences. Medically, the time from 3 to 4:00 a.m. is known as "The Hour of the Wolf" and is linked to congestive heart failure and death from chronic conditions. Spiritually, that same timeframe is known as "The Hour of The Muse," an auspicious time for inspiration, uplifting ideas, innovative art, and opportunities for wisdom-making. For Muslims, the first prayer of the day is at 4:00 a.m. Add to this the fact that Schumann Waves (the base frequency of earth, called "the earth's heartbeat") rise during this time—most crop circles in the world were and still are formed during this same hour.

Another curious find: many hospice nurses report that 80 to 88 percent of dying patients have "spirit visitors" who manifest to the left. Some nurses are quick to add that the nursing staff is taught to approach patients on their right side, so, obviously, anything "extra" would have to manifest or occur on the left. Not so. Even if no nurses are around, never were there, other-worldly souls still tend to enter "stage left," especially during a crisis or an emergency (not always, but usually). Also, when a person dies, a predominance of reports say they appear to leave via the left (again, not all but most). Same thing with most near-death experiencers. Left entrances and exits are common too with those who see "wee folk," practice healing massage, meditate, do prayer work, or experience out-of-body states. Always left? Some nurses and patients say no. Still, the majority associate left with mystical, spiritual, and other-worldly "goings on." Maybe the reason for this is because left activates the right hemisphere of the brain, which is, by its very nature, more creative and spiritually oriented.

What I discovered with things left, however, is something else . . . on earth the amino acids of all living things twist to the left; in space, most spiral galaxies rotate to the left. No big deal, you say? Well, I suggest to you that the clever tidbits I've just shared with you underscore a significant observation: the near-death experience seems to shift experiencers back to life's natural rhythms. Considering how far we have advanced as moderns on this planet, this observation is no small thing.

It takes a minimum of seven to ten years to integrate a near-death experience. That's with adults. Child experiencers take twenty to forty years.

You knew there would be a downside. Prepare yourself.

The divorce rate with adult experiencers ranges between 72 to 77 percent within the first ten years. Families, spouses, children of experiencers, expect to get back the loved one they nearly lost, not some remodeled, rewired version they no longer recognize or may have difficulty conversing with. Employers blink twice and sometimes show you the door—because either you no longer blend in, or, you suddenly know things you never did before and have absolutely no proof to establish that what you're talking about is worth listening to. Imagine the office disruption that could occur when you make few errors, work faster, do more than before, are happy and generous, and treat everyone kindly. Wonderful? Depends. This kind of switch can cause unbelievably negative cross-currents—all barbs aimed at you—for causing others to feel defensive and uncomfortable in your presence.

This actually happened to me, and, yes, I was shown the door. The scoop is, I was between jobs and went to a temp agency for part-time work. In the past I just walked in the door of such a place and was immediately assigned work. They do things differently in today's society. I had to take a test. No problem, breezed through office skills—high scores. Flunked the psychological quiz. They say you can't, but I did. Come to find out test questions are designed to measure the amount of stress you store in your body. If you don't store stress, you can't be measured; you blow the test. One other person flunked as I did. She taught yoga and stress release at a nearby college. Since neither of us had problems handling stress, we both were considered unemployable. Sound ridiculous? Yes. Utterly. Yet, *I really was still shown the door.* "We can't use you," they said. That's when I switched careers and turned my near-death research into books people could read.

NOTE TO MEDICAL AND HEALTHCARE PROFESSIONALS: have you noticed anything different when treating near-death experiencers? To a rousing chorus of "Yes we have," allow me to clarify a few things.

- *Low blood pressure* is normal for experiencers. This is not a sign of chronic fatigue syndrome, nor does it require disease treatment.

- *Less aging*—low blood pressure and looking younger go together, and are signs that cortisol (in the same class as steroids) is less present in the body. Because of this, experiencers tend to have slower responses to stress, which creates less cortisol, lowers blood pressure, and slows down the aging factor.

- *Light sensitivity*—fresh air is healthy, but be careful of excessive sunlight. Especially with the young, limit outside playtime and sports. Adults who work outdoors should consider wearing sunglasses and taking shade breaks. Too much bright light could be fatiguing and put the immune system at risk. Conversely, there are some experiencers who crave light and can't get enough of it. Such extreme reactions to light are commonplace.

- *Sound sensitivity*—a real challenge for teens and those living in larger cities that are inundated with loud sounds/music. This can be painful. Most experiencers switch to melodic music, the sounds of nature or silence.

- *Less tolerance of pharmaceuticals* means *less is more*. Tell your doctor or nurse that you are a near-death experiencer. This alerts them to a possible need to alter treatment. Assimilation is quicker for the vast majority, as it takes less of something for full effect. Seek out the mildest medication possible for your condition. Be careful with child experiencers, as substances for them are administered according to weight and age and often contain unnecessary or excessive sweeteners.

ALERT: *Children do not integrate near-death experiences.* The younger the child the more this is true. Children compensate or adjust instead. A child's job is to grow up and learn all they can. If something interferes with this or in any way hinders average development, the child will typically forget, push aside, shelve, or repress what doesn't fit or seems to get them in trouble. The majority of child experiencers grow up feeling somehow "alien," as if they neither fit their family of origin nor the local community. There are those, however, who come back utterly tuned in and knowing, with enough confidence to brush aside or stand up to parents and friends who think they are fantasizing. Learning about the near-death phenomenon and what is normal for experiencers makes a huge difference for children. And adults, too.

Electrical sensitivity can cost you a fortune. Casting aside wrist watches is one thing, but when electrical grids malfunction, light bulbs pop, equipment starts without touch, cassette recorders smoke, microphones garble, DVDs and CDs go mysteriously blank—this really catches your attention. Not to mention when smart meters, tornado and earthquake electrical effects, living near large power lines and electrical substations and generators, wipe you out; or when you try to use computers or cell phones or I-pads or "I" "E" anything. You truly feel like an alien in a strange land. There are exercises, classes you can take, helpful suggestions that enable you to fit back into our quickly-becoming-digitized-world. Still, the "stamp" of au naturale demands that we discover what we can be near and what we need to stay away from. The rest teeters on balance.

Scan that pattern of physiological and psychological aftereffects again. Do you think coming back to life is a slam dunk? Not all near-death survivors are survivors. Some are unable to bridge differences. The International Association for Near-Death Studies, during their annual conferences, make certain they have speakers and topics for the families of experiencers, and ways for "others" to learn what is normal to the phenomenon. Once families and friends have a better understanding of altered character traits and how typical they are, the collective sigh of relief people feel is palpable. If significant others are willing to listen and hear what the experiencer has to say without judgment or criticism, everyone benefits. It's amazing when this happens.

The "prize winner" for having experienced the largest number of episodes that I ever found was a man in his early forties who claimed to have had 23. Born with extreme handicaps, he was not expected to live past six months of age. He barely made it to his seventh month, died again—and again and again. Resuscitated each time. Over the years that followed this crisis pattern continued, leaving him in a wheel chair and dependent on caregivers. When I asked him why so many episodes, his answer was rather cryptic: "They're my vitamin pills. They give me the strength to keep going, so I can live out the life I was given." There were no regrets in this man; rather, an unending strength that amazed and inspired others.

You know, the wondrous tales of afterlife and the return of "betterness" can actually detract from the tough questions we need to ask:

- What do aftereffects say about neurological changes in the brain and nervous system that are supposedly impossible?

- What does the phenomenon say about consciousness itself, where it exists, what it might be?

- What about the human body and what it is capable of above and beyond enhanced faculties and the spread of awareness and knowing?

- What does the phenomenon and its aftereffects say about our current scientific models, protocols, and how we arrive at what we think we know?

- What do experiencer narratives and the research that studies them reveal about ourselves as human beings, our choices, and our reason for being?

- What does any of this say about the soul and how mind and soul interact?

We meet ourselves, our truest self, once we begin to ask bigger questions.

8

THRESHOLD

I'm saying it: the connecting factors in all incidents of break-through into higher, more spiritual states of consciousness are the same . . . as if a formula.

Doesn't matter if that breakthrough moment was sudden or took a lifetime or in what manner it occurred. Doesn't matter if the individual is a religious person, zealot, psychic, yoga master, kid, mystic, near-death experiencer, shaman, conservative traditionalist, innocent bystander, magician, idiot, criminal, or Brahma Bull rider at some rodeo in Montana.

What follows is true for every person, any age.

The span of my life, all the investigations I have done beginning at age five when I did my first double-blind study with controls (I was determined to figure out what caused the colors and textures of mud pies) . . . all of it . . . led me to the discovery of how transformation/transmutation occurs in humans beings and where it leads. For me to reveal what I discovered requires that you, dear reader, keep reading.

I'll keep things as simple as I can while approaching the subject from interesting angles, with the single goal of leading you bit by bit to some "whammies" (wake up calls) that I hope touch you as deeply as they have me.

I promised simple, so let's begin a long time ago in Egypt.

Drawings from ancient Egypt show Anubis, God of the Afterlife, weighing a person's heart against a feather upon the individual's death. Judgment: if the heart weighed more than the feather, the individual was selfish and went to the lower worlds; if the heart weighed less than the feather, the individual was selfless and went to the higher worlds.

There is a threshold. A single place. A single moment of shift in that place.

The heart decides. At the threshold.

The threshold is that boundary, that line, that space, that moment of a shift in energy where you meet the ultimate. All pass through here. Thoughts, beliefs, matter not. Legends speak of a fearsome watcher at the gate to that passageway—perhaps an animal, guide, or demon, the previously dead, or scratches inside an insane mind. Although high stress takes us to this place, even if we wished to be there, even if we prepared in advance as part of a ritual to be there, breakthrough still surprises.

The near-death experience is a threshold event. So are any of a myriad of other events that mimic near-death in the power and intensity that can be released by them to transform body, mind, and soul. I am thinking here of episodes like "Baptism of the Holy Spirit," kundalini breakthroughs, shamanic vision quests, "mountain top" revelations, bursts of radiant fire and light, being struck by spirit, ecstatic unions with God. Perhaps you can name more. Realize as you think of any, that everyday awakenings can eventually lead to this place—like involving yourself in the deeper reaches of the creative mind, developing spiritual vision, maybe through the disciplines of prayer and meditation, mindfulness techniques, selfless service, compassionate action, healing others, the "Quaker Way" of going within.

These experiences comprise the genre of transformations of consciousness, events and situations linked by similar patterns of energetics, aftereffects, and where the experience leads. And they all lead to the same endpoint: Oneness: One God, One People, One Family, One Existence, One Law, Love, One Commandment, Service, One Solution to Problems: Forgiveness. Ofttimes referred to as "The Perennial Philosophy," this experience of Oneness is much sought after, and has ever been so.

What decides and controls breakthrough at the threshold? The heart.

Do you have any idea of just how smart that heart of yours is, mine, everyone's? Science tells us that around 65 percent of heart cells are neural cells. That means the heart is a brain. With a force field shaped like a torus doughnut, the heart is so powerful it out-produces the brain 1,000 times more electrically and 5,000 times more magnetically. Our heart busily converts one form of energy into another, generating an infinite number of harmonic waves. These harmonics run throughout our bodily systems, and are so sensitive *they react to conditions seconds, sometimes minutes, before actual occurrence.* This futuristic awareness tells our heart if what's coming is positive or negative, so it can prepare itself. Our heart feels the coming event, then the brain becomes aware of it, then our eyes or senses react. The heart is literally our first responder.

Stay with me on this.

When heart energies come together, unify, higher energy fields are accessed. Feelings of love and connectedness engulf us . . . with a feeling-sense that operates like a thinking mind with an unbelievable memory. As foretold in ancient Egypt and from wise ones throughout history, a soul set free by higher heart harmonics becomes dedicated to service.

Love, or lack of it, dominates near-death, near-death-like, and higher consciousness/transformative experiences. All of them. The fullness of love, being loved, and discovering the power of love, appears to determine the overall effect such states have on experiencers and on anyone who hears experiencer stories.

Spiritually speaking you could call the whole process of threshold . . . a breakthrough into oneness and higher forms of love . . . *a soulquake* . . . because the process is literally *a power punch*.

Early in my work I recognized that what ties near-death and other transformative states together is a basic energetic . . . a power that somehow "pushes." You get a sense of this in the mythology of "the hero's journey": *Crisis* (high stress that sets the stage); *Watcher at the Gate* (facing what one most fears); *Other-worldly Journey* (an in-between space where all that is known suddenly converges, suspends, expands); *Transformation* (being forever changed by what happened); *Marked* (imprinted via a pattern of physiological and psychological aftereffects that can have lifelong consequences).

There is a formula here, and it is physically real and can lead not only to transformation, but transmutation . . . second birth or the idea of being born again.

This happened to Persian mystic Jalal ad-Din Rumi when his teacher died. Rumi was so overcome by this that he plunged into deep grief. He fled to his backyard where there was a pole. He grabbed the pole and spun around it, around and around, back and forth. As he did this, beautiful words of poetry began to flow, which his students wrote down. His followers adopted this "spinning" ritual. Seven hundred years later, we have "Whirling Dervishes" who still believe that by spinning as Rumi once did, they open themselves to God. Rumi's poetry touches the heart and uplifts the masses as much today as centuries ago.

Same thing in the dairy business. No kidding. Spin cream long enough, hard enough, back and forth, round and round, vigorously—magic happens—the cream turns into butter. I used to churn my own butter, so I know about this. No matter what you do with that butter it will never again be cream. The type of churning that created it, forever transformed the final product by imprinting the butter with the results of the spinning it endured. Similar to Rumi and that pole and the belief of Whirling Dervishes.

Excuse me for appearing to be rather crude, but, honestly, there's really no difference between what Rumi did and the butter churn. They both became "colloids" after being subjected to the rigors of a "colloidal condition."

I apologize for subjecting you to such strange terms, but . . . well . . . read on.

A threshold experience sets the stage for the possibility of a colloidal condition (that process which transmutes one property into another). The basic pattern of energetics, what comes next—breakthrough/change/aftereffects—is identical. In case you've forgotten high school science, a descriptive refresher follows.

A colloidal condition (the process itself) is where:

- forces suddenly collapse, then converge

- a momentary state of suspension results

- everything caught in that suspension expands and enlarges as antigravity is created

- inherent or unlimited potential is released

- whatever is present is imprinted (becomes permanently altered by what occurred)

- whatever is present then transmutes (takes on different characteristics)

- as reversal of motion is completed, forces are restored, suspension ends—but the imprinting (transmutation) remains

The energetics of a colloidal condition creates colloids: transmuted particles, substances, people. Should the threshold experience be intense enough, it becomes a crucible of change (a colloidal condition that creates colloids). Butter can never again be anything but butter, no matter what you do to it. Rumi's poetry and the wisdom he shared survives today untouched and unchanged from the power it continues to evoke hundreds of years later.

Another example centers around the life of Walter Russell (1871-1963). Facts about his early years are sketchy. Enough material survives in letters to indicate he was near death at the age of seven (high fever). He revived, utterly in awe of what he had seen on the Other Side. When 14 he was officially pronounced dead from black diphtheria by the attending physician. Once again, to the amazement of all, he revived—this time convinced he had entered into "at-one-ment" with God—which he said enabled him to discover the secret of healing. Every seven years thereafter he either underwent another near-death or near-death-like event, until at the age of 49, when he had an "illumination of cosmic consciousness" that lasted 39 days and nights without abating.

When he regained use of his faculties (which took quite a while), Russell penned *The Divine Iliad* (about his experience), and then spent the next six years writing *The Universal One*—a text containing drawings, charts, and revelations given to him about the universe and how it worked, covering such topics as chemistry, physics, and electromagnetics. Before his illumination, the man was a musician, writer, artist, and architect—entirely self-taught and self-supporting since the age of 14. He later corresponded with Albert Einstein about his own theory that ours is a "thought-wave" universe created for the transmission of thought." I have these books, including *The Secret of Light*, and I still marvel at the depth and detail of what he received while enveloped in light. When he died in 1963, Walter Cronkite, in the national evening news, commented on Russell's death, referring to him as the "Leonardo da Vinci of our time."

In the summer of 2009, students of Russell admitted that he was deeply into alchemy, not as per Hermetic Law; rather in accord with revelations given to him plus what he himself knew was possible. He had an invention of his tested at Westinghouse Labs back in 1927. I saw that lab report. It showed that with this invention of his (which enabled the transmutation of one element into another), such a transmutation did in fact occur. Lab officials at the time didn't quite know what to make of this, thus, no follow-ups occurred. A physicist, not knowing what Russell had accomplished, replicated that invention many years later and obtained the same results.

Most of the individuals canonized as Saints by the Catholic Church had a near-death experience as a child that redirected their growing years into paths of service and healing. The same is true of memorable psychics, inventors, ministers, spiritual teachers, and master healers—among others.

Transfiguration and transmutation—whether of people, conditions, or the very elements that make up the universe—are common themes of threshold experiences.

We were born, most of us, with the "equipment" needed to procreate, to continue our species. We were also born, all of us, with the "equipment" needed to recreate, to transform our species. Using the near-death phenomenon as an example: temporal lobes in many cases expand afterward; IQ enhancements occur as well as the spread of expanded faculties; thinking becomes more spacial, non-verbal, sensory-dynamic; creative problem solving emerges with a more active sense of what memory is; sensing multiples can open up new worlds of time and space; the higher mind develops in league with greater concerns for social justice and moral integrity, compassion; whatever is latent surfaces.

Whammy time: *the entire genre of transformative events constitutes a biological imperative, an imperative that assures the advancement of the human race to higher and higher states of consciousness.*

We were made for this—to be more, to know more, to expand.

We were made for this—to enrich and transcend the human experience.

We were made for this—to know the God of Our Being, and to see ourselves through the holy mirror God provides.

9

THE BIG PICTURE—
ADULT'S VERSION

Breakthrough journeys into the Other Worlds of spirit are acutely personal and absolutely real. No one's belief or disbelief can alter this fact.

I've said this before, still, it bears repeating: there is no one experiencer and no single experience that is more important than any other. Quoting from holy writ to validate or legitimize near-death claims accomplishes little or nothing, and serves no one. Same with claims of privyness to transcendent realms and revelations.

All of us glimpsed a small portion of The Big Picture. But, none of us saw as much as we think we did.

The greatest power that emerges from breakthrough journeys to the Other Worlds of spirit is *a collective one*—not what one person saw or heard, but the sum of the many. When you've listened to as many experiencers as I have, you take note . . . for the collective message that emerges is what speaks with the voice of thunder.

And that's what this chapter is about—revelations and understandings assembled from the thousands of adult experiencers I've had sessions with and The Big Picture that emerges from them.

What Existence Is

No question about this one: time and space exist only on the earthplane.

When you die and leave your body behind, you leave earthly constraints. Whatever seemed solid and real evaporates.

Although similar planes to the earthplane do exist and are populated by the familiar, it doesn't take long to realize that the totality of existent realms and dimensions far exceeds any number that can be counted. The various realms and dimensions range from slower, more dense vibratory fields of form to higher, finer streamers of non-energetic currents (beyond form). And that isn't all. Our universe isn't the only universe. Some experiencers report seeing life in multiples of galaxies.

No one knows how vast creation is. To an experiencer, though, existence is life, never ending and ongoing, forever and eternal.

Throughout the narratives I have heard, read about, or learned of, there does seem to be one overall, dependable, constant, consistent movement everywhere present and evenly distributed and experienced throughout all of creation—that is completely free of the distortions of time and space. This single background "constant" is *expansion and contraction*, as if the existence that exists were capable of breathing. What appears as a progression, a time-line of starts and stops and ever-changing variations, may actually be an illusion, one that helps us to keep our focus where we currently are—so we will accomplish what we came here for (or at least have an opportunity to do so), and not be distracted by whatever enables the reality we think is real to exist.

If this sounds like so much gobbledygook, compare what I am trying to convey with how television sets worked before they went digital. The picture we enjoyed seeing on the older sets, the progression of a storyline with characters acting out a script, was actually a trick of perception. What existed, what was really there, was quite literally one electron at a time (with black and white sets, and three at a time with color) fired from the back of the television tube to the screen to be illuminated as a tiny dot once it hit the screen. The continuous barrage of electrons-turned-into-dots created the appearance of images, as scanning lines (raster bars) rolled from top to bottom separating information coming in (new dots) from information fading out (old dots). You adjusted the vertical hold on your television set, not to remove strange lines appearing in the picture, but to place all screen activity within the range of your own perceptual preference. Those old television tubes were nothing more than a "gun" that fired electrons onto a screen. Your mind connected the electrons/dots into the picture images you think you saw, while totally ignoring the true reality of what actually undergirded and upheld the situation. The way television once worked, at least in our daily experience of it, was and still is a perceptual illusion.

Did this example help? I hope so. According to experiencer accounts, what exists seems to operate a lot like those old television sets. Existence itself, what really truly exists, cannot be fathomed by how it appears. There is a deeper truth.

The Realness of God

The realness of God/Allah/Deity/Source/Core (whatever name you prefer to use) becomes up close and personal like ring-tones throughout your body, mind, and soul.

Vocalized or not, you come to know: God is the one presence, the one power, the one force and source of all. God has no competitors because no reality exists outside of God. God is omnipotent (all powerful), omniscient (all knowing), and omnipresent (present everywhere). Quite simply, there is no place where God is not.

God is neither a man or a woman or a thing. God is no one's father or mother or benefactor. We use human terms of parentage to help us understand relationship—ours to God. Such personal (even neutral) pronouns serve as a matter of convenience or because of a need we have for comfort and security. We call ourselves Children of God because we do not know what else to call ourselves, and it seems as good a term to use as any. We are made in the image of God, not in the sense of physical appearance, but with respect to the power in our souls and the potential of our minds. God is Creator. We are co-creators. It would be more appropriate and more in line with truth if we called ourselves Extensions of God or, perhaps, Thoughts in The Mind of God.

While God is more than name, protocol, hierarchy, concept, or grandiosity, amazingly, God truly is as near as our next breath, as close as our next thought. We are part of God and existent within God. A belief in separation, that we could possibly exist and have our life apart from God, *is the greatest of all sins*. The belief of separation is of our own making. God has not decreed such a thing. We did this ourselves by pretending that somehow, some way, we could transcend That Which Cannot Be Transcended.

God is not dependent on our belief, for our belief or disbelief in God does not affect God—only us.

There is no one religion just as there is no "chosen" people or person, nor any single way of regarding what cannot be fully comprehended. We are all "Sons" of God in the sense that we are all souls of God's Creation, without gender, without form, without nationality, complete and whole and perfect as we explore the neverendingness of God's Wonderment. A spark from the essence of All That God Is resides in each and every one of us as an unbreakable connection, thread, or cord that ensures we remain a part of That Which We Could Never Leave.

The splendorous joy of recognizing and acknowledging our specialness, our greatness, as creations of God and as co-creators with God, is akin to being engulfed by overwhelming floodtides of God's Glorious Love.

The Big Picture

One of the overwhelming realizations experiencers face is learning that . . . *there is no sense of crime or punishment in God's Light, only the clear, complete, and total knowing that you are loved unconditionally and fully—right now, forever.*

If ever there was a big "WOW," it's this. No sermon intended here. Just that big WOW. And to back up that WOW, as an experiencer, you get another one, continuous numbers of them (as you've already seen), until you feel as if you'll explode, then more WOWs follow, until you feel flat-out stunned.

Imagine for a moment that you too are an experiencer and suddenly you've broken through the threshold and are either introduced to or slammed with truths you've probably never had to face before or, frankly, had never heard of. You may counter with "what-ifs" and "what about this" or "explain that." Doesn't do any good. No matter how loudly you protest or how demanding your challenge or how emotional your outcry, revelations keep on coming.

Truth in the Light that greets you on the Other Side is so powerful and so piercing, there is no way you could lie, exaggerate, avoid, or deny what you have done with God's gift to you, the gift of life on the earthplane with abundant opportunities to learn and develop and grow—be the best you can be. This gift, the earth life God gives us, comes with a catch: you have to give the gift back.

We cannot keep the life we have on the earthplane, not our possessions or attachments or relationships. What we can keep is our memories and our feelings of what we have integrated into our heart of hearts from the experience of being here, plus the love we have shared with others. This, what we can keep, enriches God's experience of us as well as enriching our experience of ourselves and one another. How joyful this is depends on what we did about who we are.

Each gain or loss anyone makes affects everyone else to some degree. That's because we are connected, somehow, as sparks from The Mind of God. Everything created either has a soul or is capable of being "ensouled." Because human beings contain larger portions of a soul mass than many other forms/ beings, they represent opportunities of greater diversity, challenge, and activity. Yet even animals, minerals, plants, and planets, contain degrees of ensoulment replete with intelligence, feeling, memory, and volition. Density and shape may seem to deny this, but the creative fire is ever-present, every-when.

All souls are holy in God's Light, and all souls are loved. All souls have a purpose for their existence and a reason for being who or what they are. Whatever form a soul empowers "fits" in creation's story, for each soul has a job to do, a place to fill in the greater scheme of things.

And all souls evolve. Nothing stays as it is because nothing is static, regardless of how "otherwise" conditions may appear to be. Evolution is not restricted to linear progression. It only seems so.

The drama of creation's story is unbounded—neither limited by our perception of it, nor by our ability or lack of ability to comprehend it. This drama is as stupendous as it is terrifying, as awesome as it is wonderful, as miraculous as it is mysterious, as beautiful as it is the ultimate act of all-consuming love. To witness even a glimpse of such glory, to know The Real Truth of it, leaves a mark so profound you are forever uplifted and transformed.

You return from your near-death experience *knowing* we affect each other because we are all part of each other, and that we affect all parts of creation because all parts of creation interweave and interrelate with all other parts. Any sense of aloneness or separation dissolves in The Light of such knowing.

We each matter. And we are each challenged to "wake up" and realize that we matter. Once we so awaken, our task is to act accordingly. *To know is not enough.* We must express that knowing. How we do that is up to us.

Although we are each connected to the other and to all others, we are individual in our choices, in the power of our will, and in the result or consequences of our ever having breathed a breath in the earthplane. The responsibility we have for this totality of our beingness is as freeing and exciting as it is humbling. And it represents high adventure.

The greatest fear we have in living out our earth life is not what might happen to us, but what might be expected from us if we recognized who we are.

Priorities and Values

We glorify God just by existing.

Our mission or our purpose in life reveals itself as we go along. It is not something we have to know in advance; it is simply an urge of "rightness" we follow or associate with or are open to, when we are receptive enough.

Whatever brings us closer to God or wholeness, is of value. And what does that for us is love, charity, patience, joy, faith, wisdom, knowledge, healing, laughter, sharing, cooperation, upliftment, doing for another, service, discipline, kindness, constructive effort, using our talents, lending a hand, giving a blessing, grace, forgiveness, meditation, prayer, respecting ourselves and others, happiness, harmony, melody, the pleasure of satisfaction in a job well done.

What is positive and life affirming is desirable.

Yet, negatives are not undesirable.

Fear is positive in that it protects us from harm. It fosters the gifts of caution and discernment and discrimination. Fear is only negative when we allow it to paralyze or cripple or restrict, suffocating us with "phantom enemies" of our own dread.

Anger is positive in that it motivates us and "sets the record straight." It fosters the gifts of creative force, drama, inner cleansing, and truth telling. Anger is only negative when we allow our ego to let surface on its fiery currents whatever is repressed or suppressed within the inner depths of our own psyche.

Our priorities in life depend on the choices we make and what we empower by our presence and our personality. Literally, wherever we put our attention is where we put our power.

We walk by faith, not by sight.

We live by grace, not by effort.

We exist in love, not in time or space.

The Small Stuff

What has been shared thus far is an introduction to a broader view of life and its living, a broader view that comes with this twist: "Don't sweat the small stuff." Experiencers quickly add, "It's all small stuff." (There's a lot of laughter among near-death experiencers.)

Most claim that it is their thoughts, their attitudes, and their beliefs that are the major cause of any troubles they might have had in their lives. This places personal responsibility over blame, conflict resolution over revenge, creative problem solving over dictatorial threats or demands. And they are more at ease with diversity, while displaying a greater tolerance for ambiguity and change.

The majority accept psychic abilities as soul abilities, feeling that these extensions of faculties normal to everyone actually enliven their lives, save them time and money, and add a "grace note" to relationships. Since science has established that most of the universe is either infra or ultra to our perception as humans, these psychic/intuitive "extras" are regarded as a way to access more of the electromagnetic spectrum—a way to expand the range of what is typical.

It is true that near-death and other experiencers of intensely transformative events smile often and give great hugs. Wouldn't you, if you were no longer controlled by the tyranny of time?

A brief aside: On Sunday, June 16, 2013, Philomena (Henry) Jit passed from this earth for the second time. Thirty-nine years before, while giving birth to her son via cesarean section, she died the first time. She was clinically dead for four hours, toe-tagged for delivery to the hospital morgue, when she suddenly sat up—frightening both morgue and hospital staff. I met her while I was giving talks in the

New York City area back in the late nineties. I was impressed then with her radiant glow and enthusiasm for life. Her near-death episode, typical in what she encountered, transformed her utterly.

A reminder: let's not lose sight of the millions of Philomena's around the world. They don't write best sellers. You won't see them on stage. Yet, each in their own way became living testimony to what else we are as human beings.

10

THE BIG PICTURE—
CHILDREN'S VERSION

That collective voice includes children. Since kids do not think as adults do, this chapter ranges in content, enabling you to see through their eyes. We'll begin with a killer tornado.

Todd C. Frankel, staff writer for the *St. Louis Post-Dispatch*, wrote an article datelined December 19, 2011, entitled "The Butterfly People of Joplin." In the article he quoted some of the children who were caught up in the disastrous May 22nd Joplin, Missouri, tornado that nearly wiped the thriving city off the map. The children spoke of "butterfly" people in and around the tornado itself. The kids said the butterfly people protected them. Some townsfolk claimed they were guardian angels. Others dismissed the whole thing as a child's fanciful imagination. But those who saw the phenomenon never changed their story; they believed there really were butterfly people flying around and up inside Joplin's terrible tornado, trying to help them.

I was called in on this case by Frankel because of my background in working with child experiencers of near-death states. What impressed me was the number of such sightings, and that none of the smaller children ever used the term "angel." This is significant, and alerted me to the genuineness of the phenomenon. Child experiencers never say "angel" unless previously exposed to the term by their families or friends. Little ones will instead say things like "bright ones" or "the people." The fact that the Joplin kids named the special beings who helped them "butterfly people" made sense. It was in keeping with what is typical for kids.

Ari Hallmark's book about this was introduced to the world in an online article posted May 15, 2012. Ari was six when the Joplin tornado struck, killing five in her family and leaving her in a field alone. With help from friends and relatives, she wrote *To Heaven After The Storm.* Only she and her cousin Julie survived. Ari said she was with her family members in heaven for a while. While there she saw her father Shane with hair (he had been bald all her life). He didn't have his glasses, nor were the marks of how he once wore them present. With all the media hype that later occurred, she switched terms and now calls the butterfly people angels. When I tracked down her book I spoke on the phone with several people who knew her. Both confirmed this additional piece to her story . . . *Ari somehow "knew" her parents were going to die about six months before they did.* Knowing she could not change what was about to happen, she spent the precious time she had left enjoying them. Her book, by the way, is a treasure.

There are several things to note here. First, she went to heaven with her family and saw once there that her father looked better than before. Second, she knew in advance what was about to happen. Third, she had help surviving— and so did many of Joplin's youngest— thanks to other-worldly spirit beings.

I've learned to listen very carefully to children, even the very youngest. What may seem like imagination often is not.

With little ones, what they talk about can be quite real. Don't dismiss them just because they use phrases you may not be familiar with, and, don't twist their stories around to validate how you see things.

I have no hesitancy in saying Ari Hallmark had a near-death experience.

Who's to say how "dead" she ever was? She did go to a heaven-place with her parents and grandparents and one of her cousins. And she stayed there until a spirit-type-of-being told her she must return. Although she exhibited no injuries when found in the field, she still went through what millions of kids do when at that knife's edge between life and death. Hers was indeed a threshold experience.

Some youngsters can be horribly injured, some lightly, others not at all (like Ari), yet they return from death's grip glowing and transformed. Seldom do you find a child's near-death or transformative experience lasting as long or being as complex as those experienced by teenagers and adults. Children generally have the Initial Experience (of the four patterns I discovered). These usually have only one or two, maybe three components to them, and that's it (out-of-body experiences being the most common). Aftereffects follow.

What I have noticed with children (the younger, the more pronounced), is the *exceptional maturity* they can display when relating what happened to them and what may still be happening. These experiences can peg them for life with a unique worldview and "truth-detector." It's as if they "walk to the tune of a different drummer" *before they are old enough to know what "tune" society expects them to follow.* They tend to grow up more familiar with other worlds, spiritual hierarchies, and journeys into spirit than others, and can be inclined as adults to devote their life to service, healing, or a "calling" to reach out to others (i.e., Catholic Saints, master teachers, great ministers and artists, devoted physicians). Those who don't turn in directions similar to those mentioned, can get lost and wind up going the other way— into "worlds" of depression, crime, and alcoholism. What is so crucial with children is having adults, their families and friends, simply listen to them without judgment or bullying. Give them a chance to speak their piece and act a little "different." Let them know it's okay to be like they are.

Highly recommended for kids (adults can do this too) is to *make your book*. Gather together a lot of paper, maybe some ribbon to hold the pages together. Give your book a cover and a title, then record everything you can remember before, during, and after your episode. If there are newspaper clippings, paste them in your book. If there were witnesses, ask them to write what they saw, then put that in your book, too. Compose poems, write down your thoughts and dreams, and leave blank pages at the back for future notes, maybe about certain aftereffects that catch attention. I can't begin to tell you how healing it is to "make your book." Doing so validates your experience and the quest for meaning. No electronic devices for this. All hand work. That's because of the nerve endings in your hands and the unique way they interweave and interconnect body and soul.

Child experiencers are so dear. We need to listen to our kids more. They have such amazing things to say. I did listen, deeply and long, and discovered in doing so that to a child, Truth with a capital "T" covers smaller ground and is more simply put than what an adult might say. To honor this, I offer you a summary of comments children gave me of what they learned from their near-death episode.

Bear in mind as you read this that these children have a more mature way of viewing reality than their age-mates. Imagine as you read this children's version of The Big Picture that one of those special youngsters is lecturing you about the real truth of life based on what he or she learned through dying or by coming close to death. These kids do indeed tend to lecture if allowed to, and most are confident about what they know.

Children's Version of the Big Picture

There is no afterlife— just an ongoing life stream we leave and return to as we take part in different experiences.

God exists. It doesn't matter what God is called, God is still God. And we are each part of God, always. We only think we can be separated from God. Really, we can't.

We each have a purpose in a Larger Plan, and we are important to that Plan. We each have a job to do. Large or small doesn't matter.

It doesn't matter if you know what your job is. If you follow your heart and pray about it, you'll be shown or nudged in the right direction.

Worship is important, so is an altar of some kind in your home or in your bedroom. And whatever is on your altar is holy. Church is important, too, some kind of church or place of worship, inside or outside, forest or big building— because church is God's House.

Church shouldn't put people down. Everyone has the right to ask questions and to want to know more. If a church doesn't let people do this then it isn't God's House anymore.

Prayer is powerful. You can see it and feel it. Prayer power travels in beams and when a prayer beam hits you, you feel warm and good all over.

Food tastes better if you say Grace before you eat, and have candles and flowers on the table. Most foods are okay to eat, but you need to ask the food first if it wants to be in your tummy. Sometimes the food says no. If we would listen better, we would feel better. We should listen more to our body, too. It tells us more than our head does, sometimes.

Animals are our friends. They help us learn to share and to give. Rocks are our friends, too, and so are fish and water and plants and all kinds of things. Everything is alive— that's why we need to respect our world.

We need to respect each other, too, even babies who aren't born yet.

You don't need a body to see, hear, think, feel, touch, smell, and know things. All that stuff is easy to do without a body. The only reason anyone needs a body is to grow. You can't grow if you don't have one. That's what makes a body important, and you need to take care of what you have— or it can't take care of you.

We have the families we have because we need them. Sometimes we choose our family, and sometimes we get what we get because it's our assignment and we get "brownie points" for saying yes. Other times we're just "booted" in because it's our turn.

Mistakes can be corrected. We're never stuck. We just forget how The Plan works until something happens to help us remember. We all know more than we think we do. That's one of those things we need to remember.

Life can get pretty scary. Getting in touch with the love that is inside of us can make the scary things go away. If that doesn't work, get help. None of us ask for help like we should. We think we can do everything by ourselves, but we can't.

There are always helpers around us ready to pitch in. Some wear bodies and some don't.

Work is important, so is learning. It's okay to buy things and earn money, but what's really special is helping someone, lending a hand, doing chores, cleaning things, making a home, being a friend, getting ready for tomorrow, expressing love, forgiving people. What we do for others matters more than what we do for ourselves.

You can't laugh enough, and play and create things and sing and write poems and scrunch up your nose so your face tickles. Always be loyal and truthful. Lying hurts you or someone else, sooner or later.

No one ever dies. We just trade one body for another one. Sometimes that's a happy thing to do and sometimes it's not. Whatever we experience becomes God's experience, and God never forgets a thing.

Everything is made of light. Spirit is what holds light together so it can become shapes and forms. Spirit is everywhere, like air, and it breathes, but not like our nose does. That means everything breathes. I do. You do. So does God. God's breath is what keeps the universe alive.

We are stuffed full of love 'cause God is. So's everything else. It's a wonder how many people forget that, and they forget about having a soul. We each have one, that's our perfect part. Our soul makes certain we remember who we are, so we can always make our way back to the life stream— our homey home— no matter how far away from it we travel.

One More Thing

A friend of mine and fellow near-death survivor participated in some of the most gruesome and horrific battles of the Vietnam War. He was also part of the army contingent that was the first to arrive after the massacre of Vietnamese civilians by U. S. troops at My Lai in 1968. Picking his way through the carnage, he happened upon a little girl digging a grave to bury her family. The task was hers, since she was the only family member left. My friend spoke with the child and she told him she must now do as her father had once asked of her: *look for the light on the dark side of the mountain.* "I will make a garden over the graves of my family and plant food," she explained, "so people going by will never go hungry."

Perhaps by now you understand why I said, we need to listen to our children.

11

REVELATION

Never before in all of history have we had an opportunity like we do now to examine a spiritually transforming experience through the objective lens of science.

Notice I said science, not "scientism" (the worship of science, absolute in findings). The near-death experience does this for us. Skeptics—and especially those well-meaning, well-educated stewards of the healing arts who object to anything that sounds "unreal"—have failed in their determination to brand near-death states as mere examples of drug hallucinations or oxygen deprivation or the remnants of a dying brain. The best of news sources still prefer rants against near-death studies to anything positive.

Recently, this "wall" has been blasted open by Sam Parnia, M.D. and three experiencer accounts that include extensive medical verifications.

Parnia, an expert in the newly emerging field of resuscitation medicine, wrote *Erasing Death: The Science That Is Rewriting the Boundaries Between Life and Death*. Physicians take note: techniques now exist to bring back those dead for well over an hour—*without brain damage*. The latest brain scan tests with those in coma also show that someone comatose for years can respond to questions and mind games as if their brain were fully online—indicating that consciousness may have a "sleep mode" (like a laptop computer) that can awaken at will.

In an article of his, Parnia states ". . . these survivors have gone on to provide us with remarkable yet consistent accounts of what they experienced during the period after their own deaths had started. The problem for us, as scientists adhering to the principle of objectivity while remaining unbiased, is, *What are we to do with the evidence provided to us by these millions of survivors from all over the world?*" "So by definition," he says, "there has to be some sort of 'afterlife.'"

The newest in amazing cases of near-death experiences come from Eben Alexander III, M.D. (*Proof of Heaven*); Anita Moorjani (*Dying to Be Me*); Mary C. Neal, M.D. (*To Heaven and Back*); and Colton Burpo (*Heaven is for Real*). A few more are listed at the close of this book. Millions of such cases have now been reported globally—far too many to publish. All of them, though, in ways unique to each, wake us up to a different truth than we heard before, as well as knowledge of the very real presence of a higher order to the life we live. This higher order is somehow part of and connected to an even Greater Presence.

We are on the edge now of what physicist Wolfgang Pauli once decreed: a new science is needed to explore the objective side of human consciousness and the subjective side of matter. *Not* mysticism, but a science willing to incorporate objective *and* subjective avenues to discovery, while recognizing the legitimacy of personal experience.

To this I have dedicated my work.

I've spent half my life researching near-death states. Taking into consideration my present age, that means I can remember the attack on Pearl Harbor, air-raid drills, rationing, people crying and dying. Saturday morning kid flicks always featured adventure stories, cowboy heroes, and newsreels of Hitler and his goose-steppers turning an entire country into a killing machine. I puzzled how he managed to fool the world while blinding his people to what he was really up to. And I puzzled during my early years waiting on Dad in the police station (he'd drive me home during coffee breaks), how victims of crime could justify what happened to them when they often admitted: "I just knew if I opened that door something bad would happen" or, "I had a feeling not to trust that man." I would scream in my head: if you already knew what was going to happen if you did that, why did you do it? I decided as a child that adults were stupid and I never wanted to be one when I grew up.

Guts and blood. Trauma. Secrets. Unfinished business. The mistakes we make or the puzzles we face or the questions we long to have answered—that's the fodder transformative events like near-death zero in on. What many experiencers gain privy to are the whys, the surprises, the truths hiding behind the curtain in-between what we call life and what we call death.

My reentry, back to "life as always," began at ground level after my three near-death experiences were over—relearning how to crawl, stand, walk, climb stairs, run, tell the difference between left and right, hear properly, see properly, and rebuild all my belief systems. Sensory alterations complicated the exercises I did. What I recorded of that bright sunny day in downtown Boise, when I ran an entire city block and didn't fall down, offers a good example of what I went through during the first year afterward :

Each minute sensation from my legs was received in my brain as if it were the after clap from a sonic boom. That loud, and I could both hear and feel simultaneously. If I couldn't hear a sensation then I couldn't feel it either because, for some reason unbeknownst to me, both faculties had merged. They were now equal halves of the same sensory mechanism, reverberating in shouts of feeling/sound throughout my body.

As I cried out for the joy of being able to run again, I noticed rays of energy protruding from me and spiraling out into the air. They looked like pulsating flares glinting in the sunlight.

A car honked when I wobbled off the curb into the street, feeling somewhat dazed and giddy. I jumped back and when I did, those energy flares flipped into fireworks, setting off a cascade of what appeared to be miniature rockets shooting off in all directions. I could taste it, the sun, and I could taste the satisfaction of being there standing on the sidewalk. Whatever I saw or thought about deeply had flavor, a taste. My faculties for sight, thought, and taste had also merged. Feeling/sound. Flavored sight and thought. Who in their right mind would believe any of this? Me? Anyone?

My tears of joy at being able to run rolled into wracking sobs that day, for I was overwhelmed by the strange sensing multiples that assaulted my brain. I didn't know then, but what in all probability had happened to me—the reticular activating system in my brain had opened. This system consists of a small bundle of densely packed nerve cells located in the central core of the brain stem, below the limbic system. Its job is to filter out "excessive" distractions so the brain can steady the focus you want to maintain; sorta like adjusting the lines (raster bars) in those old TV sets so what you saw was what you preferred (perceptual prejudice). I believe that so many of the "differences" experiencers undergo begin here—a literal stripping away of the old so we can be more fully present and aware of what has always been there—seemingly beyond anything we could perceive.

I could not distinguish between animate and inanimate beings/objects either—another perceptual spread. Everything was alive to me, breathing, and possessed of intelligence, volition, memory, and feeling. A funny story my daughters still tell is that when my favorite coat virtually shredded and could be relined no more, I was heart-broken, so I held a funeral service for my coat in our backyard. They howled in glee when they caught me in the act. I kept wondering what was so funny about burying my good friend, the coat. Several years passed before I figured out why the laughter.

There are no signposts along the pathway for "dealing with it," but there are precedents, stories, discoveries, and a few teachers here and there. Still, no one and nothing can make much difference until you finally realize that the only person who can ever validate you *is you, yourself.* No one else can. Once you know this, the question switches from "Is it real?" to, "What am I going to do about this?" I learned that there is a tremendous difference between the challenge to LET GO AND FLOW and the invitation to LET GO LET GOD. The differences I discovered are worth noting.

LET GO AND FLOW denotes a time when you allow yourself to be swept away on unseen tides, bereft of landmarks or guides, and subject to ever-changing floods of emotion and thought. It can be healthy to experience this type of immersion into the cosmic breath, the unbridled flow of pure energy and complete detachment, yet too much of it can lead to excessive disorientation and confusion, destroying any-thing constructive that might result.

LET GO LET GOD is an equal time of detachment and and disorientation, but putting God in charge invariably leads you to specific places, people, and events that offer a balanced and wholesome way to change and grow. Yes, landmarks alter here, too, sometimes radically, but there is a sense of direction and purpose, a steady knowing and faith; also the aftereffects are easier to stabilize.

Neither focus will save you from yourself, but while the former discards all structure as meaningless, the latter embraces whatever might be meaningful. With LET GO AND FLOW no one and nothing is in charge. With LET GO LET GOD there is direct or indirect guidance. Life structures alter with either focus, and the individual is never the same again.

When I fully embraced the God I met in death, the guid-ance I needed came gushing forth. What follows has guided me since 1977.

> *Always there is life. We cannot escape ourselves or what we have builded ourselves to be, as death ends nothing but the physical body we wear. The soul, who we are, continues.*
>
> *Each moment is precious and a moment well lived enriches all our forevers, and forever can be counted on.*
>
> *The purpose of history is not to limit our tomorrows but to free them, for, as we learn the lessons our past would teach us, we are freed from the high cost of deception and deceit, freed to rein-vent our world, not be imprisoned by it.*
>
> *The bottom line is not profit, it never was. The bottom line is service plus long-term investment in the education and the*

uplifting of others. The law of entropy only applies when greed or indifference underlies our motivation.

Enlightenment is ongoing, not a plateau we achieve, as the term describes an evolutionary shift from one phase of brain function to another, opening the way for dimensions of experience without number and realms of spirit without end.

The differing planes of heaven and hell are but stages of consciousness in The Grand Spiral Of Remembrance. We inhabit these thought form levels in an effort to cleanse ourselves as we prepare for the next phase of growth.

There is only one disease, congestion of oxygen (energy), and only one cure, circulation of oxygen (energy).

Illness has only one purpose, to deliver a message from the soul level to the personality level, for us or to someone else through us.

There are only two religions on this earth, the religion of love and the religion of fear, and everyone belongs to one or the other whether admitted or not.

The only gospel we can ever know is the experience of God in our own heart.

Love is the only standard.

Choice is the only process.

Forgiveness is the only protection anyone has, for you become whatever it is you cannot forgive.

God is.

God is love.

God as love is the only standard.

Truth can be summed in four words: One Mind, many thinkers.

Epiphany is a profound illumination of wholeness that occurs when least expected—to anyone. Truly, heaven is but a breath away. You do not have to die to find it.

End Note

Breath.

Throughout the narratives of child and adult experiencers of near-death states, throughout historical and recent accounts of people who have undergone impactful transformations of consciousness, there are countless references to the universe and all of Creation breathing. The one movement everything makes, including rocks and planets . . . the one constant that undergirds Creation and all created things . . . breathing. Not to be interpreted as spirit or air; rather, breath.

I find that at times I now breathe God. The feeling I have when this occurs is one of a slight shift into the presence of sparkling freshness. This brings great peace. I wonder . . . is all of Creation and that which is created but God contemplating God? Is the final proof of God's existence how light is able to take on mass and weight thanks to that phase/shift particle scientists have dubbed the God Particle? Is the phase/shift itself the movement of God's Breath breathing life into form?

Perhaps it's not who God is that's important, but what God is.

Perhaps . . . we need to take another breath and enjoy the sigh that follows.

12

SURPRISE

Science . . .

    . . . just observed—gravitational waves in space. This strongly suggests a Big Bang occurred so rapidly, with speeds exceeding that of light, that a fabric formed capable of warping and jiggling to accommodate ongoing inflation.

    . . . recently observed—a zero-point field that interacts with the fabric of space. This field is organized and informed, as if a data bank of information.

    . . . acknowledged that—information's carrier is DNA. It's coiled antenna follows all the rules of language and possibly that of music as well, making it readily available biologically, universally, and on all levels of memory.

    . . . finally admitted that—97 percent of once-classified-as-junk-DNA actually regulates gene function and the non-verbal, non-linear, non-local flow of information. This enables every part and particle of existence to communicate with each other.

    . . . recently illustrated that—DNA properties are fractal in nature. DNA, dubbed the "universal internet" through its quantum functions, is capable of infinite expression.

. . . *recently understands that*—fractals are infinite possibility made manifest. They form never-ending patterns of self-similar shapes that emerge from chaotic endings to rearrange themselves as new beginnings.

. . . *now knows that*—fractal geometry renders science as incomplete. Fractals free what we think exists to reveal what really exists. Science, in order to keep up with advancing knowledge, must recognize and utilize non-verbal, non-linear, non-local approaches.

Match-Mate . . .

. . . *what is experienced in near-death states and those states like them*—peel back biology and what we have come to identify as "personal." Quite suddenly, the majority of experiencers knows the sum of it, and finds themselves awash in the "love-of-belonging" that floods through every soul. Being born, living, dying . . . the life we experience shimmers throughout the journey we take into a Consciousness affixed to Creation Itself (an Intelligence that defies name or description). We find ourselves at the heart of Mystery, matching what challenges science as we embrace what exists beyond what science can define.

Match . . .

. . . *the universe is awake*—it is we who have been sleeping.

Surprise . . .

. . . *look down the center*—of a DNA double helix. You will see a perfect six-pointed star, a symbol throughout history of divinity's handiwork . . . proof of God's Eternal Presence.

13

RIDDLE

What I witnessed at the Centerpoint of Creation and Consciousness, where I believe I was when I died the third time—

Riddle . . . define love and you define God.

Hint . . . consciousness, when freed from the brain organ that receives and transmits it, understands.

Invitation . . . see where this riddle takes you.

Amen.

ABOUT THE AUTHOR

**P.M.H. ATWATER** is the author of more than 15 books, including *Future Memory, Beyond the Indigo Children, We Live Forever,* and *I Died Three Times in 1977—The Complete Story.* She has been researching the near-death phenomenon since 1978, and is considered a world authority on the subject. She is a workshop leader at major spiritual/holistic gatherings, and has addressed audiences at the International Association of Near-Death Studies, as well as the United Nations, and in numerous countries. Her books have been translated in over 12 languages. She has appeared on *Larry King Live, Regis and Kathy Lee,* and *Geraldo.* She lives in Charlottesville, Virginia.

SUGGESTED CONTACTS

Information Center about Near-Death and Near-Death-Like Experiences

International Association for Near-Death Studies (IANDS)
2741 Campus Walk Avenue, Building 500
Durham, NC 27705
(919) 383-7940
services@iands.org
www.iands.org

Training Facility for Altered States of Consciousness/
Out-of-Body Experiences

The Monroe Institute
365 Roberts Mountain Road
Faber, VA 22938
(434) 361-1500 or 1-866-881-3440
info@monroeinstitute.org
www.monroeinstitute.org

Organization for Helping People Transform Themselves—
Spiritual Awakenings

Association for Research and Enlightenment (A.R.E.)
215 67th Street
Virginia Beach, VA 23451
(757) 428-3588 or 1-800-333-4499
are@edgarcayce.org
www.EdgarCayce.org

Classes and Workshops for Children with Heightened Awareness

Profound Awareness Institute
1322 Fisher Branch Road
Marshall, NC 28753
nancy@psykids.org
www.psykids.org

Professional Support with Transformative Events and Aftereffects

American Center for the Integration of Spiritually Transformative
Experiences (ACISTE)
P. O. Box 1472
Alpine, CA 91903
(619) 445-4443
info@aciste.org
www.aciste.org

SUGGESTED READING

Books/References Already Mentioned:

Dancing Past the Dark: Distressing Near-Death Experiences. Nancy Evans Bush. Self-published through Amazon Digital Services, 2012.

Dying to be Me: My Journey from Cancer to Near Death, to True Healing. Anita Moorjani. Carlsbad, CA: Hay House, 2012

Erasing Death: The Science That is Rewriting the Boundaries Between Life and Death. Sam Parnia, M.D., with Josh Young. New York, NY: HarperCollins, 2013.

Heaven is for Real: A Little Boy's Astounding Story of His Trip to Heaven and Back. Todd Burpo (Colton's father) and Lynn Vincent. Nashville, TN: Thomas Nelson, 2010.

Life After Life. Raymond A. Moody, Jr., Ph.D., M.D. Covington, GA: Mockingbird Books, 1975.

Proof of Heaven: A Neurosurgeon's Journey into the Afterlife. Eben Alexander, M.D. New York, NY: Simon & Schuster, 2012.

The Work of Walter Russell. Contact Michael Hudax, now director of University of Science & Philosophy, P. O. Box 520, Waynesboro, VA 22980: (330) 650-0315 & 1-800-882-5683: think@philosophy.org: www.philosophy.org. Russell's books and materials are still available through this University.

To Heaven After the Storm. Ari Hallmark, with Lisa Reburn, Ph.D. Franklin, IL: Truth Book Publishers, 2012.

Credits on story of Butterfly People and Hallmark's Book to:

Todd C. Frankel, article "The Butterfly People of Joplin," published by *St. Louis Post-Dispatch*, December 19, 2011.

Carson Clark, weekend anchor and Sand Mountain Bureau Chief, WHNT News 19, Huntsville, AL—televised news story, 5-15-12, "Child Writes Book About Going To Heaven & Surviving A Tornado."

To Heaven and Back: A Doctor's Extraordinary Account of Her Death, Heaven, Angels, and Life Again: A True Story. Mary C. Neal, M.D. New York, NY: Doubleday, 2012.

Additional on Near-Death Experiences:

Closer to the Light: Learning From Children's Near-Death Experiences. Melvin Morse, M.D., with Paul Perry. New York, NY: Villard Books, 1990.

Consciousness Beyond Life: The Science of the Near-Death Experience. Pim van Lommel, M.D. New York, NY: HarperOne, 2010.

Evidence of the Afterlife: The Science of Near-Death Experiences. Jeffrey Long, M.D. with Paul Perry. New York, NY: HarperOne, 2010.

Irreducible Mind: Toward a Psychology for the 21ˢᵗ Century. Adam Crabtree, Alan Gould, Bruce Greyson, Edward E. Kelly, Emily Williams Kelly, Michael Grosso. Lanham, MD: Rowan & Littlefield, 2007.

Lessons from the Light: What We Can Learn from the Near-Death Experience. Kenneth Ring, Ph.D. and Evelyn Elsaesser-Valarino. New York, NY: Insight Books, 1998.

Making Sense of Near-Death Experiences: A Handbook for Clinicians. Mahendra Perera, Karuppiah Jagadheesan, and Anthony Peake, Editors. Philadelphia, PA: Jessica Kingsley, 2012.

Mindsight: Near-Death and Out-of-Body Experiences in the Blind. Kenneth Ring, Ph.D. and Sharon Cooper. Palto Alto, CA: William James Center for Consciousness Studies, 1999.

Science and the Near-Death Experience: How Consciousness Survives Death. Chris Carter. Rochester, VT: Inner Traditions, 2010.

The Big Book of Near-Death Experiences. (P. M. H. Atwater), International Association of Near-Death Studies. Charlottesville, VA: Rainbow Ridge Books, 2014.

The Truth in the Light. Peter Fenwick and Elizabeth Fenwick. New York, NY: Berkley Books, 1995.

The Wisdom of Near-Death Experiences, Dr. Penny Satori. United Kingdom: Watkins, 2014 (available in U.S.).

Some Books by Near-Death and Near-Death-Like Experiencers:

After the Light: What I Discovered on the Other Side of Life That Can Change Your World. Kimberly Clark Sharp. New York, NY: William Morrow, 1995.

Beyond Mile Marker 80: Choosing Joy After Tragic Loss. Jeff Olsen. Springville, UT: Plain Sight Publishing, 2014.

Embraced by the Light. Betty J. Eadie. Placerville, CA: Gold Leaf Press, 1992.

Hear His Voice: The Light's Message for Humanity: Revelations from a Woman Who Came Back from Heaven's Door Twice. Nancy Clark. Fairfield, IA: First World Publishing, 2012.

Love is the Link: A Hospice Doctor Shares Her Experience of Near-Death and Dying. Pamela M. Kircher, M.D. Burdett, NY: Larson Publications, 1995.

My Descent into Death: A Second Chance at Life. Howard Storm. New York, NY: Doubleday, 2005.

Return from Tomorrow, George C. Ritchie, Elizabeth Sherrill. Waco, TX: Chosen Books, 1978.

The Boy Who Came Back from Heaven: A Remarkable Account of Miracles, Angels, and Life Beyond, Kevin Malarkey (Alex's father). Carol Stream, IL: Tyndale Momentium, 2011.

The Day I Almost Drowned: A Child's Near-Death Experience. Kathryn Diamond. Self-published through Lulu Marketplace and Amazon.com. Can also obtain from www.rachelsmagicswing.com.

The Man Who Planted Trees: Lost Groves, Champion Trees, and an Urgent Plan to Save the Planet (about David Milarch's near-death experience and his mission to save the oldest, biggest trees). Jim Robbins. New York, NY: Spiegel & Gray, 2012.

Voyage of Purpose: Spiritual Wisdom from Near-Death Back to Life. David Bennett and Cindy Griffith-Bennett. Forres, Scotland: Findhorn Press, 2011. (Available in the United States.)

Extras

Biocentrism: How Life and Consciousness are the Keys to Understanding the Nature of the Universe, Robert Lanza, M.D. Dallas, TX: Ben Bella Books, 2010.

Harmony of the Universe: The Science Behind Healing Prayer and Spiritual Development, Andrew Glazewski, with Paul Kieniewicz. United Kingdom: White Crow Books, 2013. (Available in the U.S.)

One Mind: How Our Individual Mind is Part of a Greater Consciousness and Why It Matters. Larry Dossey, M.D.. Carlsbad, CA: Hay House, 2013/2014.

Randi's Prize: What Skeptics Say About the Paranormal, Why They Are Wrong & Why It Matters. Robert McLuhan. Walworth, South London: Matador, 2010. (Available in the United States.)

Sex, Sleep, Eat, Drink, Dream: A Day in the Life of Your Body. Jennifer Ackerman. New York, NY: Houghton Mifflin Co., 2007. (Refer to Chapter 13, page 186, for a discussion about "The Hour of the Wolf," that time between 3 to 4 a.m.)

The Human Hologram—Living Your Life in Harmony with the Unified Field. Robin Kelly, M.D. Fulton, CA: Energy Psychology, 2011.

The Great University of Life: A Soul Journey Progress Report. Foster Laverne Harding. Golden, CO: Park Point Press.

Website that contains Archive of Scientists' Transcendent Experiences: http://psychology.ucdavis.edu/tart/taste/. Charles T. Tart, Ph.D., creator.

Website for self-reporting of a near-death experience, plus extensive background information, created by Jeffrey Long, M.D. and his wife Jody Long: www.nderf.com.

RELATED TITLES

If you enjoyed *Dying to Know You*, you may also enjoy other
Rainbow Ridge titles. Read more about them at
www.rainbowridgebooks.com.

The Big Book of Near-Death Experiences
by P. M. H. Atwater

God's Message to the World: You've Got Me All Wrong
by Neale Donald Walsch

The Cosmic Internet: Explanations from the Other Side
by Frank DeMarco

Dialogue with the Devil: Enlightenment for the Unwilling
by Yves Patak

Dance of the Electric Hummingbird
by Patricia Walker

*Consciousness: Bridging the Gap between Conventional Science
and the New Super Science of Quantum Mechanics*
by Eva Herr

Messiah's Handbook: Reminders for the Advanced Soul
by Richard Bach

Inner Vegas: Creating Miracles, Abundance, and Health
by Joe Gallenberger

When the Horses Whisper
by Rosalyn Berne

Channeling Harrison
by David Young

God Within
by Patti Conklin

Lessons in Courage
by Bonnie Glass-Coffin and Oscar Miro-Quesada

Imagine Yourself Well
by Frank DeMarco

Rainbow Ridge Books publishes spiritual, metaphysical, and self-help titles, and is distributed by Square One Publishers in Garden City Park, New York.

To contact authors and editors, peruse our titles, and see submission guidelines, please visit our website at *www.rainbowridgebooks.com.*

For orders and catalogs, please call toll-free: (877) 900-BOOK.